HEIDEG(
LATER WR

Continuum *Reader's Guides*

Continuum's *Reader's Guides* are clear, concise and accessible introductions to classic works of philosophy. Each book explores the major themes, historical and philosophical context and key passages of a major philosophical text, guiding the reader toward a thorough understanding of often demanding material. Ideal for undergraduate students, the guides provide an essential resource for anyone who needs to get to grips with a philosophical text.

Reader's Guides available from Continuum

HEIDEGGER'S LATER WRITINGS

A Reader's Guide

LEE BRAVER

continuum

Continuum International Publishing Group

The Tower Building   80 Maiden Lane
11 York Road   Suite 704
London SE1 7NX   New York NY 10038

www.continuumbooks.com

British Library Cataloguing-in-Publication Data
A catalogue record for this book is available from the British Library.

ISBN: HB: 0-8264-2211-X
            978-0-8264-2211-8
    PB: 0-8264-3967-5
            978-0-8264-3967-3

Library of Congress Cataloging-in-Publication Data
A catalog record for this book is available from the
Library of Congress.

Typeset by Newgen Imaging Systems (Pvt) Ltd, Chennai, India
Printed and bound in Great Britain by MPG Books Ltd,
Bodmin, Cornwall

CONTENTS

The most difficult learning is to come to know actually and to the very foundations what we already know. Such learning, with which we are here solely concerned, demands dwelling continually on what appears to be nearest to us. (BW 276)

We are here attempting to learn thinking. We are all on the way together, and are not reproving each other. To learn means to make everything we do answer to whatever essentials address us. (WCT 14)

The burden of thought is swallowed up in the written script, unless the writing is capable of remaining, even in the script itself, a progress of thinking, a way. (WCT 49)

For my students, who question

ACKNOWLEDGMENTS

I want to thank my 'Later Heidegger' classes of 2004 and 2006 at Hiram College for their service as guinea pigs for these commentaries. My T. A.'s in particular, Jason 'Rush' Wray and Meg Shutts, gave me a lot of feedback. My gratitude goes to Bill Blattner who helped the manuscript see the light of day, to Charles Guignon for useful suggestions, and to Colin Anderson for clarifying issues concerning Greek translation. The editors at Continuum, Sarah Campbell and Tom Crick, have been a pleasure to work with, easing all difficulties and responding to inquiries with astonishing speed. I want to thank my children – Sophia, Ben and Julia – for their patience and good humour in letting me spend time on this manuscript. And my most heartfelt thanks go to my wife, Yvonne, whose support never falters.

LIST OF ABBREVIATIONS

AM	*Aristotle's 'Metaphysics Θ 1–3'*
BP	*The Basic Problems of Phenomenology*
BQ	*Basic Questions of Philosophy: Selected 'Problems' of 'Logic'*
BT	*Being and Time* (cited by English/German pagination)
BW	*Basic Writings* (only cited by BW when following references to other books)
CP	*Contributions to Philosophy* (cited by paragraph/page number)
DT	*Discourse on Thinking*
EF	*The Essence of Human Freedom: An Introduction to Philosophy*
EGT	*Early Greek Thinking*
EHP	*Elucidations of Hölderlin's Poetry*
ET	*The Essence of Truth*
FS	*Four Seminars*
HCT	*History of the Concept of Time*
HPS	*Hegel's Phenomenology of Spirit*
ID	*Identity and Difference*
IM	*An Introduction to Metaphysics*
IPR	*Introduction to Phenomenological Research*
KPM	*Kant and the Problem of Metaphysics*, 5th edn., enlarged
M	*Mindfulness*
MFL	*The Metaphysical Foundations of Logic*
N	*Nietzsche*, 4 vols. (volume denoted by Roman numeral)
OBT	*Off the Beaten Track*
OTB	*On Time and Being*
OWL	*On the Way to Language*
P	*Parmenides*
PIA	*Phenomenological Interpretations of Aristotle*
PIK	*Phenomenological Interpretation of Kant's 'Critique of Pure Reason'*
PlS	*Plato's 'Sophist'*
PLT	*Poetry, Language, Thought*

LIST OF ABBREVIATIONS

PM	*Pathmarks*
PR	*The Principle of Reason*
PT	*The Piety of Thinking*
QT	*The Question Concerning Technology and Other Essays*
STF	*Schelling's Treatise on the Essence of Human Freedom*
Sup	*Supplements: From the Earliest Essays to 'Being and Time' and Beyond*
TB	*On Time and Being*
TDP	*Towards the Definition of Philosophy*
WCT	*What Is Called Thinking?*
WIP	*What Is Philosophy?*
WT	*What Is a Thing?*
Z	*Zollikon Seminars: Protocols – Conversations – Letters*

CHAPTER 1

CONTEXT

Heidegger's later work attempts to think in the absence of some very basic assumptions that have long ruled philosophy and common sense, which is one of the reasons these writings can be so disorienting. Despite their difficulty and importance, there are surprisingly few guides to these works, especially in comparison with the number of commentaries on *Being and Time*. This lack is due in part to their obscurity, I suspect, but also to the absence of any *magnum opus* that can represent this phase of his career the way *Being and Time* stands for the early period. My solution to this problem is to write commentaries for the essays collected in the anthology, *Basic Writings*.[1] Although not assembled by Heidegger himself (he did make suggestions, see BW ix), it does a terrific job of providing important and representative essays from across his career, making it the most frequently used text for classes in English on later Heidegger.

My goal throughout has been to illuminate each essay's structure, giving readers a roadmap to enable them to find their own way through rather than simply presenting Heidegger's ideas in more straightforward prose. I want students to learn to read these dark, magnificent essays for themselves, using this guide as a ladder to be thrown away once climbed. Although Heidegger's writings may appear impenetrable at first, slow patient repeated readings repay one's efforts generously.[2] If you read the original essay carefully, then my commentary, and then the essay again, you should find it readable, with further readings yielding insights indefinitely. Wrestling with Heidegger's writings has been the most exciting intellectual adventure of my professional life, and if this commentary helps others embark on the journey, it will have achieved its purpose.

Throughout his many lectures on great philosophers, Heidegger rarely spent much time on their biographies. He once began a course on Aristotle by noting simply that, 'Aristotle was born, worked, and died',[3] and then turned to his thought. My comments will not be *quite* so brief, but neither will I delve into much detail about his life; far better accounts than I can give are readily available (see 'Notes for Further Reading' at the end of this book for suggestions).

After *Being and Time* (1927) became a sensation, Heidegger assumed the chair of philosophy at the University of Freiburg previously held by his teacher Edmund Husserl. Heidegger's writings during the 1930's center on the topic of truth; he spends a lot of time on the ancient Greeks, especially the way they set the course for Western thought's understanding of truth, but by the end of the decade he came to focus on Nietzsche as the philosopher who brought metaphysics to its end. Notoriously, he joined the Nazi Party and became rector of Freiburg University in 1933, only to resign the position less than a year later. There is some evidence that he grew disenchanted with the party (and vice versa), but he did not quit nor did he ever seriously address his participation. He was forbidden from teaching as part of the general post-war denazification, in which his former friend Karl Jaspers played a significant role. He was allowed to resume teaching in 1949, but preferred giving unofficial seminars and public talks, as well as writing essays, to teaching at a university. Technology and the enigmatic 'fourfold' are prominent topics of these last decades. He lived a long and productive life, leaving over 100 volumes in his collected writings (the *Gesamtausgabe*).

The first point that a guide to Heidegger's later writings must address is what it means to call these essays 'later'. In the years after *Being and Time* was published, Heidegger's thinking and writing style underwent a profound change which he called the '*Kehre*' or turning, splitting his career into two phases. *Being and Time* and several contemporary lecture courses are generally classified as early Heidegger, whereas everything written after the mid-thirties (or a bit earlier – people disagree about the exact date) is considered later Heidegger. Of course, the later work is hardly a static system; new topics, figures, and motifs surface virtually every decade of his career.

Both the nature and the extent of the *Kehre* are still matters of considerable debate, with many scholars arguing for more of a continuous development than a revolution. Heidegger's style certainly changed; as innovative as *Being and Time* is, it is far more conventional than what follows. Where *Being and Time* possesses a tightly structured system, almost a Kantian architectonic, the later essays often appear to be shapeless meanderings of poetic or mystical musings. Knowledgeable readers can get their bearings on the early work by relating it to its influences (primarily Kant, Husserl, Kierkegaard, and Dilthey), while the later work bears little resemblance to anything else in the canon, except perhaps the Pre-Socratic fragments that fascinated Heidegger so. Although a number of important continuities persist across the two phases, the differences are significant enough to make the *Kehre* a genuine break in my opinion. I will briefly discuss two of the most important changes.

First, the role humans play in Heidegger's thought changes substantially. He organized *Being and Time* around a 'fundamental ontology' by means of an 'existential analysis of Dasein' (55). This means that an analysis of our way of Being, called Dasein's existence, forms the beginning point for all further study, especially for the study of Being. In the book's jargon, the analysis of existence forms the foundation for ontology. As Heidegger acknowledges, this strategy resembles Kant's in his first *Critique*:[4] Kant examines our transcendental mental faculties in order to grasp the structure of phenomena since they are the source of phenomenal order, while Heidegger studies the nature of our awareness in general because this determines what we can be aware of. *Being and Time* tries to overcome traditional conceptions of subjectivity, but Heidegger comes to believe that it remained trapped within the subject-centered tradition (or at least that it lent itself too easily to this interpretation).[5] His later work abandons fundamental ontology by starting with Being rather than with us, the turn that was supposed to occur in the never published Third Division of Part One of *Being and Time*. Instead of our mode of existence shaping experience (and thus serving as its foundation), Being 'sends' or 'gives' us our contemporary way of understanding. Precisely what this means will be the topic of many of the essays in this book, but it certainly overturns one of the basic tenets of *Being and Time*.

Second, in the later work history comes to pervade everything. 'Historicity' formed one of Dasein's essential traits ('existentialia') in *Being and Time*, but these features themselves appeared to be ahistorical attributes characterizing all Dasein regardless of where or when they lived. The later work argues that both man[6] and reality change profoundly throughout history. Each historical era has its own way of understanding Being, and Heidegger spends a great deal of time reconstructing these earlier understandings of Being from representative metaphysical texts. This project resembles Hegel's study of the various historical moments of consciousness more than Kant's examination of the mind's single timeless configuration, though without Hegel's idea that history is heading towards a goal. At times Heidegger considers the epochal understandings incommensurable and so incapable of comparison, while at other times he describes the history of Being as one long decline from its glorious beginning in ancient Greece. In either case, any 'escape' from the metaphysical oblivion of Being that has reigned since Plato and Aristotle requires a radically discontinuous leap to an entirely new way of thinking rather than Hegel's organic development of an internal potential.

The essays in *Basic Writings* repeatedly visit a number of themes, so my *Guide* does so as well. Hopefully, the contexts in which these themes are placed and the nuances teased out of them have enough diversity to assuage any sense of repetitiveness. Heidegger insists on returning to the same ground repeatedly to achieve deeper insight into it rather than amassing a pile of conclusions.[7] Time and space constraints kept me from providing commentaries for all the essays in *Basic Writings*. I omit the Introduction to *Being and Time*, because that book already has so many commentaries that anyone looking for guidance can easily find it elsewhere, and the selection from *What Calls for Thinking?*, because it is an excerpt which really needs its full context for proper understanding. I have tried to make this commentary both accessible to those new to these writings and useful to more advanced readers. Most of the footnotes refer to other places in Heidegger's vast *oeuvre* where he discusses the same topic; these are meant to aid research and can be safely ignored by those just trying to make sense of the writings.

CHAPTER 2

OVERVIEW OF THEMES: WHAT IS BEING?

'For there is Being.' The primal mystery for all thinking is concealed in this phrase.

(238)

Throughout his long career, Heidegger asks a single question over and over again: the question of Being. He believes that despite their apparent diversity, all great philosophers are really dealing with this topic, just in very different ways.[1] Although this inquiry may look like a highly abstruse and abstract subject, Heidegger considers it '*the most basic and at the same time most concrete question*' (50). We are constantly using a tacit understanding of Being in all of our activities. Every time we interact with anything in any way, we are guided by an implicit sense of what it is. Since we are always interacting with beings in some way or another, we are constantly employing or, better, enacting our understanding of Being: 'Being is the ether in which man breathes' (SFT 98). Investigating it is difficult not because it is complex or abstract, but precisely because it is so near and ubiquitous, so simple and obvious.[2]

Whenever we encounter something, we experience it as a particular *kind* of thing which determines how we deal with it.[3] The kinds of actions it makes sense to do to a rock are very different from what is appropriate to do with a parent, or a painting, or the government, or an idea. We do not consciously consult a list of facts in order to decide what to do, of course, but rather live within a non-thematic knowing-how to deal with various sorts of things which underlies any thematic conceptual thinking.

All comportment toward beings carries within it an understanding of the manner and constitution of the being of the beings in question. We understand something like the *being* of beings, but we neither grasp nor know *that* we understand this being in a preconceptual way or even that it is this understanding that primarily *enables* all our comportment to beings.[4]

These broad 'categories' are the ways these entities *are*, i.e., the Being of these beings, and our understanding of them occurs in appropriately interacting with them. It is only once we have grasped the general way a particular entity is, such as to be used, that our interactions with it can be more specifically attuned to it.

We must already understand ahead of time something like tool and tool-character, in order to set about using a certain tool . . .. We understand such things – although at first and to begin with we do not pay attention to such understanding and do not even know that we understand these sorts of things . . . although we constantly exist in it.[5]

Because familiarity with these modes of Being is logically prior to interacting with beings, Heidegger sometimes calls them a form of the a priori.

A lot of Heidegger's writings are devoted to dredging up and describing these tacit ways of Be-ing that we have always known but never thought about.[6] *Being and Time* examines three ways to be which appear to be common to all cultures and historical periods: 'ready-to-hand' equipment we use in our everyday activities, 'present-at-hand' objects we study theoretically, and existence which is Dasein's or our way of Being. The main goal of the book as we have it is to lay out the way of Being belonging to Dasein (Heidegger's early term for us or, more specifically, our awareness) in new distinctive terms instead of concepts taken from other ways of Being, as philosophers have always done.[7]

Now, we can see right away that a way to be is fundamentally different from a being, yielding what Heidegger calls the onto-logical difference: 'a being is always characterized by a specific constitution of being. Such being is not itself *a* being.'[8] Ways of Be-ing are not themselves beings, although neither can they exist apart from beings, which leads to another motto: 'Being is always the Being of a being' (50). You cannot turn the corner in a busy city and suddenly run into readiness-to-hand; rather, you encounter tools which behave in a ready-to-hand manner. Being is more a verb or an adverb than a noun, how things are rather than a thing. Philosophers have traditionally viewed Being as the ground of all other beings, making it the highest being or the one that brings everything else into existence. But thinking of Being as a particular being, even the 'beingest' being such as God or a Platonic Form, commits a fundamental category mistake that Heidegger calls ontotheology since it confuses the Be-ing of beings (ontology) with the Greatest Being (theology).

The discipline of metaphysics looks beyond the variety of individual beings to examine 'the totality of beings as such with an eye to their most universal traits'.[9] It inspects beings qua beings, what makes anything be regardless of the diversity of particular entities, sifting through individual details to find their over-arching 'beingness' or the Being of beings. Whereas his early work appears to take the three contemporary ways of Being as permanent universal features for all Dasein, his later thought assigns individual understandings of Being to each era. Much of this work consists in close readings of canonical metaphysical texts in order to piece together previous ways of Being.[10] He usually divides the history of Being into three epochs: the ancient Greeks defined it as *physis*, during the Middle Ages all beings were creations of God, and in the modern period to be was to be a substance, which came to mean either being a subject or an object posited or represented by a subject.[11] Heidegger generally regards these epochal understandings as incommensurable (as in Thomas Kuhn's history of science), and comprehensive for the period they govern, making it impossible to compare different ones for accuracy or to organize them into a progressive journey towards truth (though he does sometimes trace a continuous decline). A period's understanding of Being determines what it means to be at that time, which rules all other issues. Thus, questions about correctness can only take place within a specific understanding, not across epochs.[12]

Metaphysics looks beyond individual beings to the common traits that define the Being of these beings, but it does not ask where these meanings of Being come from or why they are the way they are.[13] These meanings cannot be explained by referring to beings since they determine how we experience and understand these beings. Beings always underdetermine what we make of them. Metaphysicians often resort to ontotheological explanations: things are this way because they participate in the Forms or because God made them this way. But this just pushes the question back a step, leading us to ask why the Forms or God are such that they made everything this way. Explaining beings in terms of other beings, even transcendent ones, leads to either an infinite regress or an arbitrary halt at something unexplained.

Our normal absorbed use of beings keeps us from rising to the abstract metaphysical analysis of our contemporary beingness; pursuing this examination, however, closes off more challenging questions. Stepping back from *this* level to examine the various historical forms of beingness allows us to realize how profoundly they differ, which disrupts our usual way of unreflectively taking the present way of understanding Being for granted. Instead of being the only reasonable way of coming to grips with the world, our understanding becomes one option out of many. This is the move from beingness to what Heidegger calls variously *Seyn* (translated as Be-ing or Beying), Being itself, the truth of Being, or Being as Being. 'Metaphysics inquires into being in regard to how it determines beings as beings. Now, in another sense, the question of being is *entirely other*. It does not inquire into being insofar as it determines beings as beings; it inquires into being as being.'[14] Rather than starting from beings and asking what grounds or determines them, this investigation starts from the multiple historical understandings of Being and asks about their source in Being itself.

We have to be careful here because Heidegger is not looking for an explanation of the various forms of beingness, such as that a God crafts them. Since explanations only make sense within a particular understanding of Being, there can be no meta-epochal explanation of how or why these understandings themselves occur. Rather, the question highlights the fact that these understandings occur (that they are 'sent' or 'given' to us) as an inexplicable event which he sometimes calls *Ereignis* (variously translated as the event of appropriation, propriation, or enownment). Every time such an event happens, it ushers in a new epoch by letting beings appear in a profoundly new way.[15]

We usually pay attention to the beings that are present or, at most, to their essential way of presenting themselves (beingness), ignoring the simple fact that they present themselves to us at all. This built-in neglect is what Heidegger means when he says that Being withdraws or conceals itself in the very act of unconcealing beings. Viewing the present form of beingness as one possibility among many instead of the self-evident and inevitable Way Things Are, lets us reflect on the wondrous fact that we have an understanding of Being at all.[16]

Heidegger is trying to bring us to recollect Being, thus overcoming this long oblivion or forgetfulness of Being. He wants to help instigate a new epochal shift, one more radical than the three which have occurred so far, sometimes called the other beginning. The Greeks initiated the first beginning by going beyond merely busying themselves with beings to ask what they are in general. However, Plato and Aristotle turned this inquiry into metaphysics or philosophy by focusing on beingness and grounding beings in a higher being. This investigation has gone on for millennia, during which 'one can no longer be struck by the miracle of beings: that they are' (BQ 169). As Kant, Hegel, and Nietzsche did before him, Heidegger wants to bring metaphysics to a close.

Although he cannot describe post-metaphysical thinking in any detail, being at best in a transitional state between metaphysics and post-metaphysical thinking himself,[17] we do know that the thinking to come must be deeply historical. It acknowledges its dependence on Being for how it thinks and, since this has changed profoundly in the past, it must remain open to future transformations. Thus, the idea of a final, fixed answer to philosophical questions can no longer be a goal for finite dependent creatures like us.[18] What we find intelligible and persuasive is conditioned by our particular understanding; although we must think in tune with our present understanding, we can never forget that it remains just one possibility among many. Ultimately, this is a form of becoming aware of our presuppositions, perhaps the defining philosophical endeavour, but now with the acknowledgment that the foundations our thought rests upon can never enjoy absolute justification. In a particularly arresting phrase, our understanding of Being is a groundless ground.

Finally, thinking remains endlessly grateful for the gift we have been given. We should become explicitly aware of our openness to beings and celebrate it with wonder.

> Wonder displaces us before everything in everything – that it is and is what it is – in other words, before beings as beings . . .. This is the most simple and is the greatest . . .. The acknowledgment of beings as beings, however, is only sustained in questioning what beings as such are. This question is not a desire for explanation or for the elimination of the most unusual, that beings are what they are. On the contrary, this question is an ever purer adherence to beings in their unusualness, i.e., in primordial terms, in their pure emergence, in their unconcealedness.[19]

Although we are always in 'the clearing' in that we are always open to beings, we rarely think about it. Heidegger wants us to explicitly acknowledge it in thankful thinking, which means coming to dwell where we have always already been.[20]

CHAPTER 3

READING THE TEXT

a. What Is Metaphysics?

Asking about metaphysics represents an indirect approach to Heidegger's constant question, 'what is Being?' Since we do not know how to ask this question, much less how to answer it (44), this essay examines metaphysics, i.e., the study of beings considered simply as beings in Aristotle's definition. The title seems to promise a second-level inquiry into Being, a meta-metaphysics if you will (see M 333): instead of asking the question of Being directly, we will inquire into the inquiry itself.

Heidegger immediately disabuses the reader of any 'expectations of a discussion about metaphysics' (93). The method of phenomenology is to examine how phenomena show themselves (81), so we should find a way to let the subject matter 'introduce itself' (93). In this case, we examine the activity in question by actually engaging in it rather than just talking about it, or studying how others do it, or dictating how it ought to be done according to presupposed notions. We must find and pursue an exemplary metaphysical question to see what it shows us about the subject in general. This short preliminary section ends by outlining the three phases of the investigation: 'the unfolding of a metaphysical inquiry', elaborating it, and then 'answering it' (93). The rest of the essay neatly divides into three sections with titles reflecting these phases. As difficult as he is, Heidegger often helps readers with orienting 'sign-posts' like this.

I. THE UNFOLDING OF A METAPHYSICAL INQUIRY

The first section of the essay opens by claiming that metaphysical inquiries put the questioner into question, echoing *Being and Time*'s argument for fundamental ontology.[1] In order to get our bearings on a question as profoundly mysterious as 'what is

Being', we should begin by studying the being who is asking it, called 'Dasein' in Heidegger's early works. Our way of Being determines what kinds of thoughts we can have and what kinds of beings we can investigate, so we can start getting a sense of what an understanding of Being must be like from how we understand in general. No matter what the topic, our questioning can only take place 'from the essential position of the existence [*Dasein*] that questions' (94).

Although this strategy resembles *Being and Time*'s fundamental ontology, there is an important difference. Whereas the early work tried to uncover the permanent and universal features of all Dasein's understanding (59), now our specific historical situation plays a role. Instead of seeking ahistorical constants beneath varying historical conditions, this talk starts from the particular place and time Heidegger finds himself in – addressing the faculty of a university in the early part of the twentieth century.[2] The prominent feature of such a group is that they are scientific in the sense of the German word '*Wissenschaftlich*'; i.e., they are engaged in rigorous, disciplined study conceived more broadly than the English word 'science'.

In order to understand a metaphysical question we must understand the questioner, whose primary feature has just been revealed as being scientific; understanding this scientific question requires an investigation of science. Heidegger's description of science here sounds startlingly like his conception of phenomenology in that both study beings impartially, suspending all previously held views to let beings 'show what they are and how they are' (95). This resemblance is odd since he usually depicts science as doing just the opposite, i.e., filtering experience through rigid preconceptions.[3] Here he speaks in almost messianic terms of the sciences' potential were they true to 'their most proper intention' (94).

Science's proper goal is to study 'beings themselves – and nothing besides' (95). Science is only concerned with real things, not with imaginary beings or daydreams and certainly not with nothingness; universities do not fund Departments of Nihology. But Heidegger points out that in order to reject nothingness, science must employ it. Excluding 'the nothing' from its subject matter, as in 'nothing but beings are studied', involves precisely what is being excluded. This means that in defining itself, science 'has recourse to what it rejects' (96). This is significant because we can only use a word properly if we have some understanding of what we are speaking about;[4] thus science's claim to 'know nothing of the nothing' (96) undermines that very denial. In its self-definition as dealing only with beings, science deals with the nothing.

This argument follows thinkers like Parmenides and Spinoza in claiming that definitions necessarily involve negation. Although they appear entirely positive, definitions are actually woven out of negations because identifying something as, say, a dog simultaneously determines it as *not* a cat, *not* a kitchen, *not* a rainbow, etc. Parmenides considers this a *reductio ad absurdum* of the very possibility of distinctions: they require negation which incoherently presupposes that nothingness is real. Heidegger reverses this argument: distinctions are forms of negation which is grounded on the nothing, hence the nothing must 'exist' in some sense.[5]

This highly condensed argument stands in need of considerably more clarification and justification. The decision to open with this excursion into science might be due to his audience being made up of researchers rather than to its being the most natural way to raise the issue Heidegger wants to address.[6] He may also be trying to show that supposedly abstract and esoteric philosophical questions are not artificial impositions from a specialized discipline, but emerge naturally when we rigorously think through our everyday activities, in this case scholarship.

II. THE ELABORATION OF THE QUESTION

In any case, this discussion has yielded the metaphysical question we were seeking – 'how is it with the nothing' (96) – which the second section of the essay will now pursue. However, we immediately run into three objections that threaten to stop the inquiry before it even gets started.

1 Grammar: The very structure of the question 'what is the nothing' treats it as a being, forcing answers to assert that it is something or other (97). But whatever we end up finding out about the nothing, one thing we know is that it certainly is not a being, which suggests that all discussion of the nothing is doomed to nonsense (97). This line of thought, clearly

grasped by Heidegger, forms the basis of Rudolf Carnap's famous attack. According to Carnap, Heidegger is just exploiting a linguistic loophole by treating the logical operation of negation as a noun which, he naively assumes, must name a thing. Since both the question and any answers to it break the rules of proper usage, the whole discussion is simply meaningless.[7]

2   Intentionality: According to the phenomenological notion of intentionality, introduced by Brentano and developed by Husserl, consciousness is always consciousness of something. All of our thoughts and attitudes must be about something. But if in fact our minds are necessarily directed to beings, then thinking of the nothing appears impossible (97).

3   Finitude: The preliminary definition of the nothing as 'the negation of the totality of beings' (97) requires us first to grasp the totality of beings in order then to negate them, a task far beyond our limited intellects.[8] I cannot keep all of my CDs in my head at once; imagine trying to think of everything that is.

As in the Introduction to *Being and Time* (42–44), Heidegger is pointing out obstacles to his project only to show that they are based on presuppositions he rejects. These three objections are only valid 'assuming that in this question "logic" is of supreme importance, that the intellect is the means, and thought the way, to conceive the nothing' (97). These objections show that *reason* is incapable of reaching the nothing, but this only places the nothing beyond inquiry *entirely* if reason is our sole means to investigate matters. And now we can start to appreciate the significance of the earlier claim that metaphysical questions place the questioner in question: in order to find out if we can answer this metaphysical question about the nothing, we must examine our ability to answer questions in general. If our access to reality is entirely, or even principally, cognitive, as the vast majority of philosophers have believed, then these three objections do render the endeavor futile. We cannot think our way to the nothing so, if rational analysis is our only reliable way to pursue inquiries, we must give this one up.

The 'hermeneutic circle' gives us a preliminary reason to distrust this conclusion: our very ability to talk about the nothing, even in rejecting it, demonstrates some grasp of it, otherwise we would not know what it is we were rejecting. 'If the nothing itself is to be questioned as we have been questioning it, then it must be given beforehand. We must be able to encounter it.'[9] Our familiarity with the subject of our inquiry rests on a prior 'encounter' with it. If we could find and reactivate this experience, we could study the nothing firsthand. We have already established that it could not have come from reason, so we must examine Dasein – our way of being aware of or open to beings – for an alternate source of experience.

Rejecting philosophy's traditional focus on theoretical knowledge, Heidegger sees our access or openness to the world as multi-faceted, all of which present legitimate aspects of reality. One of *Being and Time*'s main conclusions is that we relate to beings in all sorts of ways, among which theoretical observation enjoys no primacy.[10] This view is rooted in phenomenology's commitment to take experience as it is given rather than sifting its real objective aspects out from the subjective or illusory ones according to a presupposed criterion. If, as in this case, logic proscribes an experience that we actually have (a claim that has only been intimated at this point, not demonstrated), experience trumps logic. This arrangement undermines 'the reigning and never-challenged doctrine of "logic"'.[11] We have to be careful not to caricature Heidegger; he is not *rejecting* rationality or logic as genuine and important modes of access to beings. Rather, he is insisting that our relation to reality possesses other dimensions which have been severely neglected or even demonized throughout the history of philosophy as subjective distortions which present only obstacles to our quest to understand reality. He writes a few years later, '"logic" and "the logical" are simply not *the* ways to define thinking without further ado, as if nothing else were possible' (IM 127).

Heidegger calls the aspect of our awareness that he will focus on here '*die Befindlichkeit der Stimmung*', awkwardly translated as 'the founding mode of attunement' (100); Krell later amended his translation to the somewhat more natural-sounding, 'finding ourselves attuned' (PM 87). *Stimmung* means mood as well as the tuning of a musical instrument (see 128 footnote), suggesting a metaphorical relationship between the two. If we are in a bad mood, certain events will depress us whereas the same events can be laughed off in a better mood; similarly, the same note that sounds sad when the instrument is tuned to a minor key can sound cheerful in a major key. Heidegger coins the noun '*Befindlichkeit*' from the German expression, '*Wie Befinden Sie sich?*' This phrase functions like 'how are you doing' but its literal translation would be 'how do you find yourself', so '*Befindlichkeit*' means something like finding oneself in a particular state or frame of mind. The term emphasizes our passivity in that we do not *decide* to be in a particular mood but simply *find* that we are so inclined.

Heidegger argues that our mood 'determines us through and through';[12] it affects which details we tune into or tune out and how we interpret them. Moods do not compromise thinking's proper functioning as an external source of corruption, but are deeply intertwined with thinking. As Heidegger states some years later, 'man is not a rational creature who . . . in addition to thinking and willing is equipped with feelings; . . . rather, the state of feeling is original, although in such a way that thinking and willing belong together with it.'[13] Whereas philosophers have traditionally considered reason and emotions distinct faculties and sought to preserve the purity of the former from contamination by the latter, Heidegger views our grasp of the world as a holistic blend.

We have arrived at an important juncture in the essay so let's pause and review. So far we have seen that:

1 Science claims to focus exclusively on beings, rejecting the nothing.
2 Logic denies reason's ability to inquire into either the nothing or beings as a whole.
3 We must have had some encounter with the nothing in order to be able to ask about or reject it, undermining #1.
4 Moods constitute an essential aspect, even 'the basic occurrence' of Dasein or our ability to question and understand (100).

In order now to answer our metaphysical question, we must reactivate our encounter with the nothing (#3) to give us an experience of it which will guide our analysis. Since reason cannot produce this experience (#2), we should look to a mood to supply the needed data (#4), disrupting philosophy's exclusive reliance on reason.

According to the initial definition of the nothing as the negation of all beings (98), we encounter the nothing by grasping the totality of beings and then negating it, a grasp that proved beyond reason's ability. Heidegger now solves this problem by distinguishing 'between *comprehending* the whole of beings in themselves and *finding oneself* in the midst of beings as a whole. The former is impossible in principle. The latter happens all the time in our existence' (99, italics added). We cannot rationally comprehend beings as a whole, but a *Befindlichkeit* of this is commonplace. If a mood can provide access to phenomena relevant to an investigation that reason cannot, this would show that reason does not deserve its long-held status as the only legitimate way to know reality.[14] This move represents the culmination of the progressive demotion of reason throughout the nineteenth century, from Kant's proscribing its ability to know reality in-itself and prioritization of the practical, to Kierkegaard's emphasis on paradoxical faith and passion in decision-making, to Nietzsche's focus on the body and will. Heidegger takes the fight into reason's inner sanctuary and sacred ground: metaphysics.[15]

Heidegger now provides brief phenomenological descriptions of three fundamental moods which supply an encounter with the nothing: namely, boredom, love, and anxiety. Love is passed over very quickly, while boredom receives more attention and, as in *Being and Time* (§40), anxiety enjoys a lengthy discussion. Still guided by the initial definition of the nothing as the negation of the totality of beings, he starts with love and boredom as presenting beings as a whole for us to negate. However, notice that this definition was introduced as elucidating 'a word we rattle off every day . . . blanched with the anemic pallor of the obvious' (98), a description that hardly inspires confidence.

And in fact, the experience of boredom leads Heidegger to abandon this definition (100). If the nothing resulted from our negation of the whole of beings, it would be the product of the mind's activity. We would be able to bring it about voluntarily rather than passively finding ourselves in it as a *Befindlichkeit*. Instead of negating beings as a whole, Heidegger finds the 'correspondingly original mood' that directly 'reveals the nothing' in anxiety.[16]

Acquiring this direct experience represents another turning point in the essay since we now have the evidence needed to answer our metaphysical question (101). This examination ends up refuting many of the conclusions reached so far, reinforcing the superiority of phenomenological descriptions over logical argumentation. In particular, the experience undermines the stark contrast between beings as a whole and the nothing that logic had demanded. In place of this sharp division, anxiety teaches us that being and nothingness intermingle. The significance of this claim, Heidegger admits, is far from obvious: 'in anxiety the nothing is encountered at one with beings as a whole. What does this "at one with" mean?' (102). Clearing up this matter will require an answer to the metaphysical question that ends both the first and second sections of the essay, 'how is it with the nothing?' (96, 101).

III. THE RESPONSE TO THE QUESTION

The first section of the essay uncovered an exemplary metaphysical question ('how is it with the nothing?'), the second covered the right way to conduct the inquiry (via careful examination of a direct experience of the nothing in anxiety), and now the final section of the essay will discover the true nature of the nothing and how it relates to Dasein. Although we were expecting to examine either beings as a whole or the nothing separately, experience reveals that boredom[17] and anxiety present the two mixed together. In these moods, we encounter beings as a whole but modified by the nothing; the desires and projects that normally keep us interested[18] in the world find no purchase.

When we are profoundly bored, that is, not bored by a particular thing like a book or movie (which Heidegger would call 'ontic' boredom) but just plain bored, all the things we usually enjoy seem bland, colorless, uninviting. They do not vanish, of course; in fact, they are oppressively present. We see the phone, but there is no one we want to talk to. The TV sits there but whatever the programs, there is really nothing on. Nothing attracts us: books and magazines do not call out to be read; games do not entice us to play. Entertainments usually draw us in but now they repel our attempts to lose ourselves in them.[19] And this is how boredom imparts a sense of beings as a whole: we get a sense of all things in that none of them can divert us while we are stuck in this 'muffling fog' of 'remarkable indifference' (99). In a later conversation, Heidegger describes it like this: 'in genuine boredom, one is not only bored because of a definite thing, but one is bored in general. That means that nothing whatsoever is of interest to oneself' (Z 208).

Following Kierkegaard, Heidegger distinguishes anxiety from fear, which is an ontic mood.[20] We fear specific beings such as a threatening dog. Here the threat is localized, understandable, and offers at least possible escape. When we fear a particular entity, other objects are not frightening and can even be attractive; we welcome the arrival of the police or a door we can hide behind. This state retains differentiations among beings: some are frightening, some helpful, and many neutral. Anxiety, on the other hand, has a peculiar 'indeterminateness'.[21] It is not a specific being that makes us anxious but a nebulous sense of discomfort, of things not being quite right.

Moreover, *all* beings have the same character at these times. As in boredom, 'all things and we ourselves sink into indifference'.[22] We can still see and think about them but they no longer matter to us, which is how boredom and anxiety reveal the nothing as intertwined with beings as a whole. Rather than the complete absence or simple negation of everything, we experience the nothing as a modification of everything that Heidegger calls 'nihilation'. One of the effects of this modification is that 'in its nihilation the nothing directs us precisely toward beings' (104). Let's contrast this state with our usual, non-anxious way of life.

Normally we encounter beings within what *Being and Time* calls 'worldhood', i.e., the context of means-ends relations that orient and guide our mundane interactions. We understand gasoline as what we use to fuel the car in order to drive to the store to buy a cake for the birthday party . . .. These chains are anchored on the roles we use to define ourselves; ultimately, I take all the actions needed to put on a nice birthday party for my kids because I want to be a good father. My project lays out the field of significance or worldhood in which are embedded all relevant things and actions. We navigate these chains of use and meaning so effortlessly that most of the time we are not even aware of them.[23] A competent driver pays little attention to her car as long as it is functioning smoothly; she thinks about where she is going, what she will do when she gets there, or her mind just wanders.

In *Being and Time*, Heidegger calls this withdrawal from attention 'inconspicuousness'[24] and he shows how it characterizes most of our everyday activities, lulling us into 'auto-pilot' most of the time. 'We usually lose ourselves altogether among beings' (104) which, taken as a whole, results in 'the oblivious passing of our lives' (BP 264). But this absorption gets disrupted when the things we are using break down; the car crashes in on the driver's daydream for instance when it sputters and starts spewing smoke. Localized breakdowns light up the particular chain of usage they belong to, jolting us awake to pay attention to what we are doing. Lighting up beings as a whole, however, requires the kind of universal breakdown that occurs in fundamental moods, especially anxiety: 'the *world as world* is disclosed first and foremost by anxiety.'[25]

In Heidegger's usage, anxiety is the creeping sense that our activities are meaningless so that, as in boredom, they stop appealing to us. 'We can get no hold on things' (101) as they lie slack and uninteresting. Nothing '"says" anything any longer. Environmental entities no longer have any involvement. The world in which I exist has sunk into insignificance.'[26] Although it can strike out of the blue with no particular provocation,[27] contemplating one's mortality can easily trigger this overwhelming sense of insignificance (see HCT 291). What is the point of going to class or working out or even getting out of bed if I am just going to die someday? Who will care whether or not I am a good father 100 years from now when I along with everyone I know will be dead? In the shadow of this thought, activities and their relevant paraphernalia seem worthless because the projects supporting them no longer matter.[28]

Although this experience is horribly suffocating, like all fundamental moods it can reveal essential truths if we stay with it rather than fleeing back to 'the comfortable enjoyment of tranquilized bustle'.[29] Heidegger discusses two specific lessons we can learn from anxiety. First, it solves the riddle of how beings as a whole can be interlaced with nothingness by presenting everything (beings as a whole) as not mattering (emotionally nullified). All significance has drained away: 'in anxiety beings as a whole become superfluous.'[30] Like Hegel, Heidegger gives negation a much broader meaning than the role allowed by strict logic,[31] including these emotional cancellations in which everything appears altered, 'sink[ing] into indifference', 'receding', 'oppressive', 'repelling'.

Second, by stripping away the significance that things normally enjoy, anxiety achieves the goal of metaphysics since Aristotle, revealing being simply *qua* being: nihilation 'brings Da-sein for the first time before beings as such'.[32] Now, 'beings as such' do not represent true reality, as if our usual meaningful experience were illusory or merely subjective; such a distinction would violate phenomenology's commitment to taking reality as it presents itself in experience.[33] Seeing something just as a being means viewing a car, for instance, not as a way to get to the store, or a monthly expense, or a source of pollution, or even a car, but just as something that *is*. This stripping away of all use-meanings, which Heidegger calls nihilation,

> discloses these beings in their full but heretofore concealed strangeness as what is radically other – with respect to the nothing. In the clear night of the nothing of anxiety the original openness of beings as such arises: that they are beings – and not nothing.[34]

With their usual significance removed, we confront naked beings as just being there; the double negation that they are not nothing produces the very powerful positive recognition that they are. It is terribly uncomfortable though because we have nothing to do with them, no context to make sense of them or put them in their place;[35] we usually flee from anxiety by occupying ourselves with something (104).

This revelation of beings as such has a further consequence. *Being and Time* defines Dasein as being-in-the-world because (among other things) our identity is made out of our basic projects (being a good father) which in turn are pursued or enacted by appropriately using chains of tools (driving to the store to get the cake). 'Each one of us is what he pursues and cares for. In everyday terms, we understand ourselves and our existence by way of the activities we pursue and the things we take care of.'[36] We are who we are by carrying out our projects through the relevant equipment so, as strange as it might sound, 'Dasein *is* its world existingly.'[37] Normally, this integration allows the inconspicuousness of equipment to spread to ourselves as well, but when our goals break down in anxiety, our normal ways of defining ourselves also stop functioning. My role of being a professor organizes my world by revealing philosophy books and computers as useful and relevant, dung beetles and ice skates not so much. In anxiety I do not care for my projects, letting my world fall slack in insignificance. The roles that usually define who I am and what I do no longer feel like they belong to or *are* me, and without these self-defining projects and activities, who am I? We 'slip away from ourselves' (101).

Just as anxiety strips away their mundane meanings to reveal beings as such, so sloughing off our usual identities can 'complete the transformation of man into his Da-sein that every instance of anxiety occasions in us'.[38] It is only when we are prevented from diving into the world that we perceive the incredibly simple fact that it manifests itself to us or, correlatively, that we are open to it. Our openness to beings' manifestation represents something like the essence of Dasein: 'revealing [beings] – far from being merely incidental – is also the basic occurrence of our Da-sein.'[39] Only beings as such remain, and 'in the altogether unsettling [*unheimlich*] experience of this hovering where there is nothing to hold onto, pure Da-sein is all that is still there.'[40] This suspension of content – when 'our concernful awaiting finds nothing in terms of which it might be able to understand itself' (BT 393/343) – is what allows me to become aware of my awareness. It is when we cannot lose ourselves among beings that we can find our self in Being. This represents the culmination of Heidegger's initial claim that metaphysical questions place the questioner in question (93). The experience of beings as such brought on by the question of the nothing brings us face to face with our selves as such, or pure Dasein.

Heidegger then follows the essentialist or perfectionist line of argument that, in Aristotle's terms, once we find our *ergon* or essential activity we should perform it with *arête* or excellence.

> This peculiar impoverishment which sets in with respect to ourselves in this 'it is boring for one' first *brings* the *self* in all its nakedness *to itself* as the self that *is there* and has taken over the being-there of its Da-sein. For what purpose? *To be that Da-sein.*[41]

The fundamental project that emerges when all specific projects have been suspended is to 'shoulder once more his very Dasein, that he *explicitly and properly* take this Dasein upon himself.'[42] This qualification, that we now take up our being-there 'explicitly and properly' (*eigentlich*, 'authentically'), is key; anxiety is what allows us to become aware of and consciously embrace our openness which is always there but which we never really think about.[43]

Wonder is the attitude or attunement appropriate to taking up one's Dasein, i.e., the way to be aware of awareness with *arête*. The nothing's nihilation strips beings of their familiar use-meanings so that, as strange, they can strike us and stop our taking them for granted.[44] Wonder allows us to view our openness or ability to be aware, which we usually take for granted, as extraordinary.[45] In its many forms,[46] this represents the later work's heir to authenticity.

Wonder can be evoked in many ways; fittingly, the end of 'What Is Metaphysics?' shows how it can both provoke and emerge from metaphysical inquiry. Heidegger states that 'only on the ground of wonder – the revelation of the nothing – does the "why?" loom before us' (109), invoking Plato and Aristotle's agreement that philosophy arises from wonder. Competently employing beings takes them for granted, rendering them inconspicuous; it is only when they are estranged from their normal meaning that we wonder what and why they are. He calls the particular 'why' question that ends the essay 'the basic question of metaphysics which the nothing compels: Why are there beings at all, and why not rather nothing?' (110). The nothing 'compels' this question by revealing beings as superfluous; noticing their simple thereness provokes us to question it: why are they there? Once we explicitly think *that* Being is, the path is open to ask *why* it is.

Although this is a traditional metaphysical question, Heidegger is not posing it in the standard way. He is not seeking a reason or explanation for why reality is there, such as its divine cause. That kind of answer would commit the mistake he calls 'ontotheology' by explaining Being or the simple thereness of everything by a specific being; this does not help since any cause still presupposes Being by being there as well.[47] Instead of a request for information, this question is meant to alter the questioner's focus or attunement. Engaging in the inquiry should result in a transformation, not a fact.[48]

Wondering why there are beings is one way to become aware *that* there are beings (which means that there is Being) and that we are aware of them; it helps us become who we are, Da-sein. Our Da-sein is our openness and, like fundamental moods, asking the why question draws our attention to this openness so that we can celebrate it. As he says a few years later, the question

> prevents us, in our questioning, from beginning directly with beings as unquestionably given . . . . Instead, these beings are held out in a questioning manner into the possibility of not-Being . . . . With our question we establish ourselves among beings in such a way that they forfeit their self-evidence *as beings* . . . . Our Dasein, too, as it questions, comes into suspense.[49]

Bracketing our various preoccupations with beings reveals this openness as our *ergon*, the essential activity or function that makes us Dasein. Heidegger praises both Plato and Kant[50] for grasping that 'metaphysics belongs to the "nature of man".'[51] Since what it means to be Dasein is to be aware of beings, becoming aware of this awareness represents the highest actualization of our essence or form (to continue using Aristotelian terms that Heidegger would not approve of).[52]

The title asks 'what is metaphysics', a question which, the first paragraph informs us, can only be answered by asking a particular metaphysical question (93). Reflection on our present situation as scientific researchers studying nothing but beings raises the question of the nothing, which shows how putting ourselves in question 'transposes' us into metaphysics. The nothing in turn 'compels' the 'basic question of metaphysics' in the essay's final sentence (110). By bringing our fundamental openness to beings itself into the open, this question lets us become who we are, completing our 'transformation' into Dasein. Thus, 'metaphysics is the basic occurrence of Dasein' (109).

STUDY QUESTIONS

1 So, what is metaphysics?
2 What kind of answer can we get to the question, why is there anything instead of nothing? What is wrong with an answer like, God created the world out of beneficence?
3 How does this essay challenge reason or logic? Is Heidegger really a misologist (a hater of reason)? How fair is Carnap's objection?

b. On the Essence of Truth

The topic of truth is extremely important to Heidegger's later work, figuring prominently in his '*Kehre*' or change in thought (see 231). This essay, however, is a disorienting piece of writing for several reasons. First, it takes the form of an extended chain of thinking built by repeatedly introducing new terms and linking them to ideas and terms established earlier in the essay. Second, whereas *Being and Time* drops standard philosophical terms like 'man' in order to avoid the traditional meanings they carry, 'On the Essence of Truth' retains traditional terms like 'freedom' and 'essence' but uses them in ways that seem unrelated to their usual meanings, which can cause considerable confusion. Third, Heidegger switches to the perspective of common sense or traditional philosophy several times without alerting the reader of this change of voice. Instead of presenting the reader with a set of polished conclusions that look like they sprung from his head wholly formed, Heidegger shows how he wrestles with the issue, including some mis-steps which get retracted. Although confusing, this presents a more honest depiction of the process of thought which can teach us how to think rather than just telling us what Heidegger thought.[53]

Once you see the essay as a kind of conversation Heidegger is having with himself, and you suspend the usual meanings of words like 'essence', 'truth', and 'freedom', the essay actually follows a neat and tight line of thought. It is extremely dense, however, often covering important and difficult steps in just a couple of pages. Although he announces the moves he is making quite directly, they go by quickly; like all of Heidegger's writings, this work requires slow patient reading.

The essay's first sentence announces that 'our topic is the *essence* of truth' (115), which appears too abstract and general to be useful (116). Note, however, that it is common sense that poses this objection. Common sense blocks philosophical questioning by assuring us that we already know as much as we need to about such an 'obvious' topic. Rather than posing useless questions about the essence of truth, we should work towards acquiring practical truths (116). But, according to one of Heidegger's favorite arguments,[54] seeking specific truths requires that we already understand what truth is, that is, that we grasp its essence. Since common sense is employing 'The Usual Concept of Truth', we must examine this more closely.

I. THE USUAL CONCEPT OF TRUTH

Like Hegel before him, Heidegger points out that the ordinary sense of truth applies not just to assertions but to things as well. Gold is true if it is in accord with what it is supposed to be, i.e., genuine gold, while an assertion is true if it accords with the state of affairs it describes. The sentence 'The cat is on the mat' is true if and only if the cat is actually on the mat. Whether applied to objects or propositions, truth gets defined in terms of accordance. Although cashed out in somewhat different terms at different times, truth has long been defined as some sort of correspondence or accordance, which gets spelled out in terms of correctness.[55] In order to understand truth, then, we must come to grips with these notions.

II. THE INNER POSSIBILITY OF ACCORDANCE

Although philosophers generally take the notion of accordance for granted when defining truth, it is actually quite hard to spell out what it consists in and how it is possible. While it is easy to see how things of the same type such as two five-mark coins can be in accord with each other – they look alike, can buy the same items, etc. – statements and things are fundamentally different types of beings. A vocalization appears to have little to nothing in common with a physical object, so what does it mean to say that they are in accord? Thus, citing correspondence to explain truth only distracts us from the emperor's nudity. Even granting this traditional definition of truth, which Heidegger does up to a point,[56] it does little to illuminate truth unless it itself gets clarified.

These questions defy the 'resistance which the "obvious" has' (116) by showing that in fact we do not understand how statements can be in accord with matters (120). Although common sense and tradition reassure us that correspondence is 'the essence of truth', Heidegger concludes (in a lecture series from 1928) that 'the definition of truth as *adaequatio* is the starting point, not yet the answer'.[57]

Rejecting the traditional understanding of essence as the defining characteristics shared by a set of objects of the same type,[58] Heidegger defines essence as 'the ground of the inner possibility of what is initially and generally admitted as known' (123). This resembles Kant's transcendental inquiries into the conditions of the possibility of something assumed to be valid, such as scientific knowledge in the first *Critique*. Here it is the traditional conception of truth as correspondence between statement and world that Heidegger accepts as given, but asks how it is possible. The essence of truth he is seeking means the enabling condition or ground for making assertions about beings and checking their accuracy.

Asserting something about something, describing a state of affairs in a way that can be true or false, is a behavior directed towards something.[59] Saying that two coins are lying on the table is a way of comporting ourselves towards them which, of course, requires that we be aware of them. We have to notice them as potential subjects of assertion ('hey, there is something on the table'), inspect them to determine their identity ('ah, they are five-mark coins'), and then possibly review the situation to check the correctness or adequate correspondence of what we have asserted ('yes, I got it right – those really are five-mark coins lying on the table'). From the beginning to the end of this process – and it is a process rather than a static relationship between parallel sets of organized elements – we have to be 'open' to these beings calling attention to themselves in specific ways. This condition is so simple and basic that it usually escapes our notice, but it is 'The Inner Possibility of Accordance'.

In order to make or check assertions, in order to do anything at all, we must be aware of beings in some way. As Heidegger says a few years later, 'if our representations and assertions – e.g., the statement, "The stone is hard" – are supposed to conform to the object, then this being, the stone itself, must be accessible in advance: in order to present itself as a standard and measure for the conformity with it. In short, the being . . . must be out in the open.'[60] Only on the basis of an open comportment, i.e., a way of behaving that lets something present itself to us, can we make statements about it or verify that statements correspond to it. It is in this 'open region' (121) or clearing that beings and statements 'present themselves' (122), making comparison and accordance between such dissimilar entities possible.

If the openness of comportment is the necessary condition of correspondence truth, then it is truth's 'essence' in the sense that it enables truth to occur. 'If the correctness (truth) of statements becomes possible only through this openness of comportment, then what first makes correctness possible must with more original right be taken as the essence of truth.'[61] Only if the cat presents herself to me, and presents herself as on-the-mat, can I make the true statement that 'the cat is on the mat' or check its veracity. This means that the traditional placement of truth only in statements no longer holds. 'Truth does not originally reside in the proposition' (122), but rather in the unconcealment of beings. Making and checking correct statements depends upon things being manifest, so this manifestness is a more appropriate locus of truth than the parasitic statements.

Section One ended by looking into the condition for the possibility of the traditional notion of truth as correspondence, revealed in the following section to be our opening comportment, and now Section Two closes by asking about the condition for the possibility of *that* condition. What enables this open comportment to beings which allows us to become aware of them and, thereby, make correct assertions about them?

III. THE GROUND OF THE POSSIBILITY OF CORRECTNESS

Section Three opens with an obscurely worded but fascinating question: 'whence does the presentative statement receive the directive to conform to the object and to accord by way of correctness?' (123). I take it that Heidegger is asking the same astonishing question as Nietzsche: '*what* in us really wants "truth"?... Suppose we want truth: *why not rather* untruth?'[62] It is a startling question, one that is hard even to see as a real question: why do we value the truth? Why are our relations to beings generally organized around and oriented towards accurate descriptions of them? Obviously people can and do lie or create fiction, but the vast majority of the time we strive to describe the world the way it is without even considering the alternative. By default, we 'bind ourselves' to beings by trying to make our statements conform to reality. Why? As strange as the question is, it merely extends philosophy's constant ambition to examine all assumptions.

Heidegger answers this surprising question with an admittedly odd word-choice: freedom is why we tend to tell and value truth as well as, answering the question posed at the end of Section Two, the reason we are able to have open comportments. He briefly summarizes the three steps made so far in order to show how this latest link fits into the chain he has forged:'[2] the openness of comportment as the inner condition of [1] the possibility of correctness is grounded in [3] freedom' (123, all bracketed numbers added). The essay started with [1] 'The Usual Concept of Truth' as correctness, and then showed in Section Two that its 'essence' or 'Inner Condition' lies in [2] 'the openness of comportment'. Now Section Three is demonstrating that [2] comportment, or behavior that takes notice of beings, is itself grounded in or made possible by [3] freedom, with the conclusion (again, given his sense of 'essence') that '*the essence of truth is freedom*'.[63]

Now, Heidegger cannot mean the traditional understanding of freedom as the ability to choose one's actions without external constraint.[64] Grounding truth in *this* kind of freedom would lead to the obvious absurdity that humans simply decide what is true; despite caricatures, Heidegger explicitly rejects this view.[65] However, common sense again insists that we stick with the traditional ideas or 'preconceptions' we started with, rather than examining or redefining them. In this case, freedom gets its meaning from man: 'freedom is a property of man. The essence of freedom neither needs nor allows any further questioning. Everyone knows what man is' (124).

IV. THE ESSENCE OF FREEDOM

Heidegger immediately disrupts this reassurance with an admonishment that we should take to heart whenever we read his writings: 'indication of the essential connection between truth as correctness and freedom uproots those preconceptions – granted of course that we are prepared for a transformation of thinking' (124). Much of what Heidegger says sounds strange when interpreted according to traditional meanings, but his goal is precisely to challenge and transform these ways of thinking. *Being and Time*'s strategy of using the term 'Dasein' instead of standard terms like 'man' or 'consciousness' is less confusing because 'Dasein' has little conceptual baggage of its own; it offers more of a blank canvas which can hold an entirely new sense with little interference. However, when successful, this new strategy of taking over and radically redefining customary terms can more effectively provoke 'a transformation of thinking', that is, a change in the way we have always thought about these ideas. Since freedom has traditionally been considered a fundamental property of man, examining freedom anew leads to a deeper examination of man (124).

Heidegger defines freedom as 'letting beings be'[66] or '*being free* for what is opened up in an open region' (123). He often calls this open region 'the clearing' (*das Lichtung*) in a metaphor inspired by his frequent forest hikes. Walking through dense dark woods with limited visibility, one can suddenly come into an open place where trees are 'lighter' or thinner, allowing light to stream in and giving things room to display themselves. One of Heidegger's fundamental ideas is that Da-sein or man is like a clearing in the midst of reality: we are the there or the '*Da*' where beings can show themselves, letting them be seen and thought about. Uncovering the conditions for the possibility of our speech and behavior and our overall truth-orientation leads to this ultimate condition:

> the reflection on what correctness genuinely is . . . leads us to that which makes it possible in the first place and is the ground of this possibility. For a representation to be able to conform to beings as normative, the beings must, *prior* to this conformity and on behalf of it, show themselves to it and thus already stand in the open . . .. This open region and its

openness constitute the ground of the possibility of the correctness of a representation (BQ 174).

The 'irruption' (95) of this sphere of awareness within which beings can become manifest is the most extraordinary event that could ever happen, and Heidegger constantly tries to make us appreciate it. Here, this openness is conceived as the necessary presupposition or enabling ground (i.e., the 'essence') of [2] our ability to interact with beings and of [3] truth as correspondence. Da-sein, being the there or place where things come to appearance, is the 'concealed essential ground of man' as well as 'the originally essential domain of truth'.[67] Since this 'freedom' is what allows us to be what we are, it is more fitting to say that we are a property of freedom than that it is a property of us.[68]

Heidegger now highlights the etymology of 'existence', the name of Dasein's mode of Being in *Being and Time*, by spelling it 'ek-sistence', meaning standing outside oneself. He rejects the picture of the mind residing in an internal theatre, only receiving sensory representations of the world at an irreducible distance from it for the more phenomenologically accurate description of ourselves as always already outside our mind, out in the world, amongst beings. On this exposure to beings rests all of our comportment, so freedom, truth, and man must all be understood anew in terms of this essence.

Letting beings be, the new sense of freedom, means allowing beings into clearing to manifest themselves freely, without forcing them into preconceived molds. We are constantly letting beings into the clearing in our diverse dealings with them, but our normal busyness does not really let beings be themselves. In tune with common sense's assurances that we know all there is to know about various phenomena, and so do not need to think any further about them, 'precisely in the leveling and planing of this omniscience, this mere knowing, the openedness of beings gets flattened out'.[69] We tend to assimilate everything we encounter to a few familiar traditional horizons, stubbornly imposing a Procrustean bed of preconceptions even when inappropriate.[70] *Being and Time* (as we have it) consists largely in showing the inappropriateness of analysing humans with the perspective of things or tools, while the first section of 'The Origin of the Work of Art' demonstrates these perspectives' inadequacy for artworks. As with phenomenology (see 81), the first step of letting-be is suspending our preconceptions to allow beings to show us what they are like (125).

In addition to this ontic attitude of patient attention to things, letting-be also occurs at the ontological level of openness itself as an 'engagement in the disclosure of beings as such' (126). Although all of our comportment takes place within the open region or clearing, we ignore the clearing to focus on the things cleared. Have you ever stopped in the middle of running errands to contemplate the simple fact that you are aware? How much more often do we just 'phase out', losing thematic awareness of the car we are driving or the pen we are using, snapping out of it only when a snag is hit or the job is done? Our awareness dims down in our mundane routine where we know our way around so well that we need pay little attention; everything just fades away inconspicuously.

Although most of our comportments to or interactions with beings narrow our exposure down to what is familiar and useful while ignoring the open region, philosophy can both lift our conceptual blinders and light up the openness. 'The ek-sistence of historical man begins at that moment when the first thinker takes a questioning stand with regard to the unconcealment of beings by asking: what are beings? In this question unconcealment is experienced for the first time.'[71] A question like this, lacking both utility and a familiar method of answering it, withdraws us from ontic dealings with individual entities to let beings as a whole shimmer into conspicuous appearance, vividly lighting up the utterly simple fact that there *are* beings and that we are aware of them. When this occurs, 'beings themselves are expressly drawn up into their unconcealment and conserved in it' (126). Liberation from ontic busyness opens the space for *ontological* engagement, i.e., explicitly attending to the clearing where we do not just experience unconcealed beings, but maintain awareness of their unconcealment.[72] It is the vital asking of the question rather than any possible answer to it that represents 'the fulfillment and consummation of the essence of truth in the sense of the disclosure of beings' (127).

And now we have answered the opening question of Section Three: why are we oriented to correctly representing beings as they are? What it means to be man (in Heidegger's technical sense) is to comport oneself towards beings, to reside within the open region interacting with beings in various ways; we are being-directed beings.[73] That is why Da-sein – being the there or the clearing – is our 'essence' in the sense of enabling condition: only contact with things and other people lets us be men. This free letting-be or opening up of a clearing orients all of our comportments towards beings.[74] Ek-sistence itself – our direct-edness towards beings – inclines us to the unconcealing of them; that is what we do. Revealing beings through assertions is one way to perform the unconcealing of beings[75] which forms our most basic way of Be-ing.[76] Letting beings be, allowing them to manifest fully as they are, represents the 'fulfillment and consummation' (127) or the flourishing (128) of the unconcealment we are always doing.

After uncovering these deeper levels of truth, the last paragraph of Section Four turns to the question of untruth. Although semblance and distortion are initially attributed to man's freedom, Heidegger has already ruled out the idea that we control truth (123–4). His new conception of truth requires a rethinking of untruth as well, with the specific outcome that the two belong together (128).

V. THE ESSENCE OF TRUTH

Once more, Heidegger gives a brief recap of the ground covered so far (128). Ek-sistent disclosure or standing outside of ourselves exposed to beings is what enables us to experience them and thus make true statements about them, making freedom the essence of truth. Our comportments flourish when they let beings be, i.e., cultivate entities' own ways of manifesting.

A new topic now arises: attunement. As discussed in 'What is Metaphysics?', 'attunement' refers to both moods and the tuning of a musical instrument. Various moods tune us in to different facets or aspects of the world and determine in what key events strike us: in a celebratory mood nothing can bring me down, whereas in an irritable mood everything annoys, even news that would normally make me happy. Our attunement predetermines the general way we react to what we encounter, prevailing throughout all of our comportments (129). As in 'What is Metaphysics?', moods put us in touch with beings as a whole in a way that reason cannot.[77]

Here the primary contrast is between attunements' disclosure of beings as a whole and comportments' interactions with specific entities. Since interactions focus on individual beings, they exclude everything else (129–30). Whereas my good mood orients my reactions to *whatever* happens (beings as a whole), changing my car's oil narrows my attention to just what is relevant to the job (a few specific beings). Antarctica, e.g., does not enter my awareness during this process at all and, unlike my cheerful mood, working on my car in no way orients my attitude towards Antarctica should it arise. My car and Antarctica bear no relationship to each other whatsoever, leaving the continent, and virtually everything else in the universe, in the dark while I take care of the oil. Since freedom takes place in specific comportments which only spotlight relevant beings, it necessarily conceals everything else; there is no comportment that would not conceal.

VI. UNTRUTH AS CONCEALING

The above discussion shows how truth and untruth belong together ontically or in terms of individual beings; we now turn to the ontological side. Here we find concealment at the very heart of revealing (130). First, Heidegger argues that a complete shadowless grasp of every aspect of something is not just unattainable by our finite minds, but is actually incoherent. The way unconcealment works is that when one aspect of something comes to light, its other aspects as well as beings as a whole fade into the shadows.[78] Due to the very nature of focus, bringing one thing into the foreground of one's attention displaces all else to the background.

Second, perception and action naturally conceal unconcealment itself because we pay attention to what is unconcealed rather than the fact that it is unconcealed.

> In order to bring into view what resides in a visual field, the visual field itself must precisely light up first, so that it might illuminate what resides within it; however, it cannot and may not be seen explicitly. The field of view, ἀλήθεια [*alētheia*], *must* in a certain sense be overlooked.[79]

As he likes to translate Heraclitus' saying, Being loves to hide. Heidegger returns to this topic – the forgetfulness or oblivion of

Being – over and over again throughout his career, always trying to turn our attention to the presentation of beings. The specific conclusion about truth here is that, 'letting-be is intrinsically at the same time a concealing'.[80]

Heidegger is particularly interested in the way *this concealing itself* gets concealed. When we focus on the object of our concern, e.g., the car's oil, we lose awareness of everything else, but we do not *realize* that we are oblivious of everything else. The rest of the universe is so far from my thoughts that I am not even aware that I am not aware of it; this concealment gets concealed in what he calls the mystery.[81] Like much in Heidegger, the phrasing sounds confusing but actually describes a phenomenon we encounter all the time. There are times when we forget something but we are fully aware that we have forgotten it: 'now where did I put my keys?' A piece of information is missing but its identity is outlined by what we do remember. Then there are times when we forget something so completely we do not even remember that we have forgotten it, until that shocking recall: 'Oh, no! I was supposed to meet my friend for dinner last night! I *totally* forgot!' Although this phenomenon prepares the ground for what Heidegger will condemn, it forms 'the proper' or 'primordial nonessence of truth' (130, 131); it is a necessary part of truth rather than an unfortunate side-effect we should avoid.

I want to spend a little time on the single complete paragraph on page 131 since it represents a turning point in the essay,[82] gathering up the ideas from the first half before laying out the topics that will occupy the rest of the essay. The paragraph begins with Section Four's connection of freedom and letting-be as well as their foundational character. Anything we can do to or with beings is grounded in our ek-sistent freedom or openness to the world. Despite this inherent orientation towards unconcealing, we also have a tendency toward concealing which conceals itself in the mystery. Every unconcealing simultaneously conceals but, as discussed in Section Five, we are not aware of this ubiquitous concealing. A forgottenness which itself has been forgotten pervades the whole process.

Section Six focuses on the mystery – i.e., the fact that we are not aware that we are not aware of the vast majority of beings or beings as a whole – and now Heidegger starts laying the ground for Section Seven by showing how this mystery leads to 'errancy'.

By and large, I know my way around beings, what is appropriate to do to or with them, and I need look no farther than these standard ways of seeing and using things.[83] Although this mastery is integral to our social nature and is required for our comportments, Heidegger worries that these expectations based on long familiarity blind us to everything that falls outside them. This facile understanding lays down guard-rails that allow us to glide through our daily routine with minimal attention. We go on auto-pilot since we know what a fork is for, what an apple looks like, basically what various beings are. These pre-established horizons perpetuate themselves by assimilating any new experiences to what is already known.[84] Common sense capitalizes on this insistence on what is already known to reject any inquiries that challenge the accepted view.

Heidegger recoils from such 'omniscience' achieved through neglect because it blocks everything beyond what is familiar and useful.[85] Driven by fads and desires, our horizons shrink to what we already know, leaving our lives empty of worth, dignity, and nobility. Heidegger links the mistaken idea that we can infuse our lives with meaning by ourselves to our forgetting that Being is the real source of our understanding and meaning. Modern man willfully '*in-sists*, i.e., holds fast to what is offered by beings, as if they were open of and in themselves' (132), or as if we could construct our openness to them by our own efforts.

VII. UNTRUTH AS ERRANCY

Section Seven turns from untruth as concealing to errancy. Erring unites ek-sistant exposure to beings, the mystery as the foregrounding of a particular set of beings against the unnoticed background of beings as a whole, and in-sistent taking beings the way they initially present themselves without questioning further. In-sisting takes what we already understand about a being to exhaust its meaning, concealing the concealment of other possibilities by denying that there are any others. The entities might display profoundly new aspects within different horizons, but I will never find out if I refuse to budge from the tried and true. Scientism – the idea that only science accurately describes reality so that whatever does not fit into its concepts cannot be fully real – is a contemporary form of insistence. Minimally, ek-sistence means just being exposed to beings so that we can become aware of them, but its highest form remains exposed to fundamentally new ways of thinking, even about the most familiar objects and ideas like truth. This essay (which literally means to make an experimental attempt) pursues this ideal of openness, fighting common sense as it 'uproots ... preconceptions – granted of course that we are prepared for a transformation of thinking'.[86]

The mystery conceals this concealment: we generally are not aware that we are not aware of the vast majority of beings or alternate facets of the beings we encounter since neither informs our immediate activities. Untruth belongs with truth because concealing is inevitable; it is the flip side of unconcealment, not an unfortunate situation we have fallen into. The idea of getting rid of untruth once and for all to breathe the pure air of unadulterated truth is conceptually incoherent on Heidegger's scheme.

If man cannot get rid of untruth as unconcealing or errancy, man can at least become aware of them (134). We should recognize that we conceal aspects of the beings we focus on, as well as all the beings that we are not focusing on, and that we tend to conceal this very concealing. The most familiar ways we experience a being do not exhaust its Being, even if we generally act as if they did. My pen for instance has many different ways of Being: it is a writing implement, a cog in our capitalist economy, a piece of matter that obeys the laws of physics, and beautiful. We need to stop in-sisting that the familiar useful modes exhaust all that there is, so that we can stay ready to ex-pose ourselves to new perspectives. One of the virtues of art is that it brings to the surface alternate aspects of beings that we rarely see.

This mystical-phenomenological attitude Heidegger is trying to instill lets beings be. It patiently attends to beings until new aspects start showing themselves, formerly unseen features shyly poking through the familiar ones, so to speak. Anyone can experience this: just sit and stare at a familiar object like an apple for a full ten minutes. After a few impatient minutes ('I know what an apple is!'), unnoticed details begin to emerge, forcing the realization that you have never *really* looked at one before. This grateful, meditative cultivation of appearance is the quasi-ethical attitude Heidegger is pointing us towards (126). This conservation of openness makes us most ourselves, most Dasein, the being through whom beings can be themselves.

Perhaps we cannot constantly maintain such sensitivity (though I suspect that Zen *satori* might be something like this), but we can at least keep in mind that our horizons are inherently limited and remain ready for the new.

VIII. PHILOSOPHY AND THE QUESTION OF TRUTH

Heidegger now connects this attitude to philosophy, in particular to 'the question of the *Being* of beings'.[87] This returns to the idea broached in Section Four that philosophical questions about beings as a whole help bring about our highest form of ek-sistence. Since then we have discovered that 'man errs' (133) or falls away from this questioning stance in which beings are expressly held in their unconcealment by insisting that we know, making genuine inquiry unnecessary (135). Throughout the essay common sense has repeatedly tried to convince us to turn back, to stop questioning and rest content with knowledge suited to our normal activities.

Philosophy on the other hand is 'intrinsically discordant' (135). It acts as a gadfly irritatingly challenging what we 'know' to be the truth, the whole truth, and the only truth. In particular, philosophy is the one discipline (perhaps along with art) that recognizes the ever-present structurally necessary concealments.[88] Heideggerian philosophy acknowledges the mystery, i.e., the concealment that is necessary to unconcealment, making final conclusive answers impossible. He gives up the traditional ideal of absolutely secure knowledge that settles matters once and for all. Given his understanding of truth as intertwined with untruth at its heart and of human understanding as continually capable of revealing new facets, his 'epistemological' ideal embraces the ineradicable concealments involved in all knowing.[89] This is one reason why Heidegger consistently values questions above answers.

IX. NOTE

The final sentence of Section Nine claims that this essay aims at 'a transformation of its relatedness to Being' (138) rather than a set of conclusions. Heidegger does not seek The Right Answer since this would only perpetuate the in-sistent concealment of other possibilities. Instead, he wants to change our relation to Being from forgetful taking for granted to grateful cultivation.[90]

We are always already within the truth of Being or the clearing, but we need to become explicitly aware of it and its concomitant concealment.

Whereas most disciplines in-sist upon their particular horizon, working within their presupposed and unquestioned understanding of reality and how to study it, Heidegger considers philosophy unique in that it takes these very horizons as its subject matter.[91] At its best, philosophy is committed to challenging all presuppositions, to continually reexamining its assumptions and traditional doctrines, always remaining open to deeply re-forming its ways of thinking which then instigate transformations of our horizons. Being can always send a new understanding, so we need to stay humbly open to what appears to us.[92]

1 How does Heidegger understand truth? Why is unconcealment the essence of truth as correspondence?
2 How is untruth inextricably linked to truth?
3 Explain insistence and ek-sistence. How does errancy forget Being?

c. The Origin of the Work of Art

'The Origin of the Work of Art' is the longest essay in *Basic Writings*, and one of the most difficult. It is a sprawling, explorative essay that twists and turns as it covers a number of topics, obscuring its overall structure. It is also one of Heidegger's greatest works, dealing with many subjects central to his later thought in a fascinating way. I have returned to this essay again and again, always finding new ideas hidden in the thickets.

Like many of Heidegger's writings, this inquiry is organized around a 'what is X' question, here 'what is art?' And, again as usual, Heidegger spends a lot of time preparing the ground for the question, seeking the appropriate way to ask it before actually posing it. Heeding the phenomenological motto 'to the things themselves', we must examine actual works of art if we are to determine what art is (144). But this strategy immediately entangles us in a circle since we first have to know what art is in order to pick out works of art for our investigation to study.[93] Instead of an obstacle to overcome or avoid, Heidegger considers this 'hermeneutic' circularity part of the very nature of thinking, even finding it beneficial.[94] In terms taken from *Being and Time*, our pre-ontological or unthematic understanding (see 54) of what art is enables us to select artworks, which in turn can help us articulate and develop our initial understanding. Rather than preventing us from learning, as Meno's paradox has it, this circle enables us to discover the nature of art by examining artworks across the essay's three sections.

I. THING AND WORK

Heidegger begins his inspection of artworks by noting that, whatever else they might be, artworks are things: they take up space, occupy specific locations, and can be moved about like coal or potatoes. He narrows this feature down to a 'thingly aspect', what we would usually call the work's material: 'something stony in a work of architecture, wooden in a carving, coloured in a painting' (145). A work of art is more than just a lump or pile of material, of course, so something like meaning or beauty must get added to the mere stuff. Since artworks are at least partially things, we will examine the nature of things and then try to figure out how artworks differ from them, which takes us into the first section of the essay appropriately titled, 'Thing and Work'.

This section begins by stating the guiding question of this new phase of the inquiry: 'what in truth is the thing, so far as it is a thing? When we inquire in this way, our aim is to come to know the thing-being (thingness) of the thing' (146). Notice, however, that this is *not* actually the question being asked. Heidegger says that he's asking what a thing is 'so far as it is a thing' in order to discover 'the thingly character of the thing', i.e., studying things as a distinct region of beings carefully separated from all others. But in fact he is asking what a thing is *insofar as it is an artwork*, as stated in the preceding paragraph (146). The working hypothesis of this section is that an artwork is a thing imbued with an additional quality and, reciprocally, that things are artworks which lack something. Despite how Heidegger describes his method, his approach actually mixes categories by defining artworks in terms of things rather than examining each on its own terms.

Traditional metaphysics studies being *qua* being, i.e., the most general features that all beings share beneath superficial diversity. Heidegger's teacher in phenomenology Husserl argues that careful attention to our experience reveals profound differences among a number of basic types of beings, differences which our descriptions of reality must acknowledge through 'regional ontology'. Getting rid of variations in order to find 'true being' underneath is like, in Wittgenstein's memorable image, pulling the leaves off an artichoke to get at its real essence when, among other things, the artichoke *is* its leaves. Heidegger is committed to maintaining heterogeneous regions without reducing them to each other or to one basic kind of being.[95] Indeed, *Being and Time* presents a detailed description of three ways of Being with the insistence that ours (Dasein) requires its own distinct set of concepts, although it has traditionally been defined by categories borrowed from the other two.[96] 'The Origin of the Work of Art' is committed to this fidelity to diversity regarding the regions of things, equipment, and artworks.

The first section of 'The Origin' can be read as a *reductio* of reductionism. Heidegger says that he is asking about the thing 'so far as it is a thing', while he is really looking at things as truncated artworks or an element in a work of art. This means understanding one region by means of a different one instead of going 'to the artwork itself'. Heidegger then compounds this error by turning to traditional conceptions of thingness to relieve us of 'the tedious labour' of seeking it on our own (148). While important, studying historical views can never take the place of examining things for ourselves; the 'destruction' of the tradition occurs via a dialogue between earlier thought and our own experience.[97] Heidegger leads us down this dead-end (a partial translation of '*Holzwege*', the title of the book that originally held this essay), I believe, to let us see his thoughts evolve rather than just handing over fully-formed conclusions. Thinking along with the essay functions as a kind of apprenticeship, 'assuming that thinking is a craft'.[98]

The first section works through three traditional interpretations of thingness, all explaining regions of Being in terms of each other. The first views things as 'substance with its accidents' (149) or nonessential characteristics, a view championed by Aristotle and Locke. After listing a thing's properties, e.g., my cup's colour and shape, the question arises: *what is it* that is grey, five inches tall, etc.? What is the thing that possesses these characteristics? The answer is the sub-stance that literally 'stands under' and supports the features (150).

Heidegger points out that the subject-predicate grammar of our language lends this theory plausibility. The sentence 'The cup is grey', grammatically separates or articulates greyness from the cup in order to attribute the predicate to the subject, implicitly portraying the thing as distinct from its characteristics.[99] He quickly concludes that this definition distorts thingness by imposing an alien and inappropriate conceptual scheme onto it (151). Importantly, we discover this inadequacy not from a logical objection, but from 'attentive dwelling within the sphere of things'.[100] This careful alertness to the way things present themselves to us is Heidegger's version of phenomenology, which can never be replaced by historical views or reason's demands. We never encounter substances with accidents in our normal dealings with things, hence such an unfaithful description of experience must be rejected.

We can avoid 'assaulting' our subject 'by granting the thing, as it were, a free field to display its thingly character directly' (151). This suggests that we should describe how we actually experience things rather than focusing on traditional definitions but, instead of doing this, Heidegger moves on to the second interpretation of the thing as the unity of sensory qualities (151). I think this refers to 'phenomenalism', Berkeley's removal of substances from substance ontology which leaves bundles of sensible qualities. The cup is just the sum of greyness, five-inches-tallness, cylindricality, etc., with any mysterious entity beneath the perceived qualities an unnecessary and empirically unsupportable hypothesis.

Once again, the theory receives a phenomenological refutation. We experience a significant world populated by grey cups and cloak-wearing people, not bare, meaningless sensations (like empiricists' patches of colour) waiting to be interpreted. 'We never really first perceive a throng of sensations, e.g., tones and noises, in the appearance of things – as this thing-concept alleges; rather we hear the storm whistling in the chimney.'[101] Phenomenalism artificially separates experience into two distinct steps – bare perception of sensory data and its subsequent interpretation into meaningful patterns. But these only separate in very unusual circumstances such as moments of shock or bafflement; for the most part we live in a meaningful world stocked the familiar entities we know and love.

The third and final definition of the thing as 'formed matter' (152) returns us to the initial discussion of artworks' thingly aspect as their material. Giving form to matter seems to fit artistic creation, like a sculptor giving a block of marble the shape of a person, but these concepts actually come from equipment, a *third* type of beings (154). A tool's purpose determines what material to build it out of and how to shape it; an axe with no edge, or one made of glass or pasta would not cut well. We began our search for the nature of artworks by studying things, which was bad enough, but now our inquiry has propelled us into a third region of Being. Heidegger puts the three into an obscure organization in which each region shares a feature with one other which the third lacks, 'assuming that such a calculated ordering of them is permissible' (155).

I think that this ordering is in fact not permissible. Each type of Being should be studied on its own, not constructed from pieces cut out of the others in a kind of Frankenstein ontology, and each kind of being should be examined directly rather than leafing through traditional theories. 'This long-familiar mode of thought preconceives all immediate experience of beings . . .. Prevailing thing-concepts obstruct the way toward the thingly character of the thing' (156). Theories from the history of philosophy invade mundane experience, determining how we think about reality even when (as here) they are not borne out by our experience.[102]

Putting aside, 'bracketing', or 'destroying' these preconceptions is no easy task. As a form of genealogy, studying their history reveals them to be contingent views rather than natural, necessary, and intrinsic features of reality, which lets us challenge them.[103] The categories' appearance of self-evidence leads us to apply them to all beings in the same way.[104] Conversely, dredging up and phenomenologically refuting these preconceptions clears the way to see how various beings reveal themselves. In a second invocation of phenomenology, he says that we must suspend all these preconceptions of thingness to see it for ourselves (157).

But instead of following his own advice and turning to an actual artwork, Heidegger now proposes a new strategy based on the 'calculated ordering' of the three regions which actually compounds the problem. Because equipment partakes of both of the other regions, we will first search for the equipmental character of equipment in hope that it will shed light on things and works; 'we must only avoid making thing and work prematurely into subspecies of equipment' (158). The warning is futile because the attempt to understand thing and work by way of equipment builds this error into the investigation. Understanding artworks via things failed but, instead of heeding his own calls to examine artworks directly, he now proposes to double the error by defining both things and artworks in terms of equipment: 'the piece of equipment is half thing' and 'half artwork' (155).

Heidegger does not study a real piece of equipment but casually announces that he will examine a pair of shoes featured in a painting by Van Gogh (158). Bells should go off in your head – he is going to look at a work of art! The promise issued at the beginning of the essay to inspect works of art directly (144) is now getting fulfilled, almost by accident. If phenomenology is right to insist on the importance of this kind of encounter, the essay should undergo a significant change at this point.

The goal of describing the essence of equipment actually presents a problem for Heidegger. *Being and Time* defines ready-to-hand equipment as 'inconspicuous', meaning that while it is being used, a tool recedes from our attention.[105] As long as your car is running smoothly you pay little to no attention to it, thinking instead about what you will do when you arrive, or just zoning out. However, when we do explicitly think about the tool, it changes into a present-at-hand thing.[106] Try writing a sentence while focusing on your pen: it is harder and less skillful than when you just let it 'withdraw' into the task.

Studying the shoes then faces a dilemma. On the one hand, we have to catch equipment while it is being equipment, which happens during use (159). But precisely at this point tools are inconspicuous and therefore hard to examine. On the other hand, explicitly focusing on them changes them from equipment to inert present-at-hand objects. So, use enables them to be equipment ('the peasant woman wears her shoes in the field. Only here are they what they are'), but the users must not pay attention to them if they are to maintain their smooth equipmental functioning ('they are all the more genuinely so, the less the peasant woman thinks about the shoes while she is at work, or looks at them at all, or is even aware of them' (159)). A philosopher can study the shoes, but only at the price of halting their fluid performance and reducing them to present-at-hand things, thereby eliminating precisely what she wanted to study. 'And yet' (159), the painting somehow eludes this dilemma to make the shoes available for direct examination as they really are. In Heidegger's terms, the artwork effects the truth of the shoes.

Van Gogh's painting is an occurrence of truth or, as Heidegger likes to translate the Greek word '*alētheia*', unconcealment, by revealing a particular being in its mode of Being, i.e., the way it is. In the artwork, 'this being emerges into the unconcealment of its Being' which, in the case of equipment like the shoes, means that, 'the equipmentality of equipment first expressly comes to the fore through the work and only in the work'.[107] Both the peasant wearing the shoes and the philosophical observer have a tacit (or pre-ontological) understanding of equipmentality, as shown by their ability to use tools appropriately, but neither can 'expressly' articulate it for the reasons noted above. Artworks are privileged sites of truth by steering between use, which cannot thematically grasp equipment, and theoretical comprehension, which misrepresents the nature of equipment, to successfully present equipmentality to us.

In showing us this mode of Being, the artwork reveals its own because its mode *is* such showing, 'the disclosure of the particular being in its Being, the happening of truth'.[108] Heidegger spent fifteen pages futilely trying to define thingness by means of theories, 'and yet' looking at an artwork immediately reveals the essence of equipmentality. Just as 'What Is Metaphysics?' demonstrates how moods impart insights inaccessible to reason,[109] so here artworks deliver what reason could not. Like every form of revealing, reason shows us some facets of reality while concealing others, and Heidegger frequently demonstrates how much philosophy has missed by focusing exclusively on this one mode of access. Moods and artworks also conceal, of course, but we have had twenty-five centuries to plumb reason's depths; it is time to find out what else there is.

By looking at an artwork, we have discovered that art works as a site of truth (162). Although aesthetics has traditionally focused on beauty rather than truth, we will see that Heidegger connects these concepts. A beautiful artwork is like an exceptionally successful mini-clearing, in that it reveals beings in a particularly enlightening way.

And now Heidegger recognizes that his previous method of inquiry was fatally flawed 'because we asked, not about the work, but half about a thing and half about equipment' (164). If we return to the initial point that started us on the path of thingness – that artworks are made out of something – we now know that we must cast it in terms distinct to art rather than in concepts borrowed from things or equipment (165). He even stops calling this feature thingly, since words from other regions inevitably sneak their conceptual baggage across the border into the new region.[110] A whole constellation of new terms (such as earth, world, strife, and rift) springs up in order to get at artworks *as artworks* rather than as variations of things or equipment. I take this to be the moral of the first section: in principle, thingly or equipmental concepts cannot grasp artworks; we must understand art by way of art and from examining artworks.

II. THE WORK AND TRUTH

We have discovered that the essence of art is to be a site for truth. Now we have to come to grips with Heidegger's understanding of truth, and work out a distinct horizon or conceptual scheme for art which can explain how it effects this truth, especially since philosophers from Plato to Nietzsche have portrayed art and truth as mutually exclusive. The second section's title, 'The Work and Truth', announces that it will investigate what truth is and how works instigate it (165).

The most obvious account would be that art depicts reality and the accuracy of its depiction depends on how well the representation matches its subject. Paintings can correspond to the world in roughly the same way that propositions do if what they picture exists or occurred the way they show it;[111] a painting of a cat on a mat is true if and only if that particular cat was on that particular mat in that posture at that time in that manner. Despite the correspondence theory's self-evidence and distinguished

46

pedigree[112] (or perhaps because of them), Heidegger rejects applying this conception of truth to art.[113]

While not exactly wrong, correspondence cannot fully explain truth since it rests on a deeper condition, namely unconcealment. Sentences or paintings can only correspond to facts if we can become aware of them as potential objects of representation. In an argument that appears in many of Heidegger's writings, unconcealment must occur in order for us to notice a state of affairs, represent it, and check the accuracy of a representation.

> Correctness in representation – stands and falls with truth as unconcealment of beings . . .. With all our correct representations we would get nowhere, we could not even presuppose that there already is manifest something to which we can conform ourselves, unless the unconcealment of beings had already exposed us to, placed us in that cleared realm in which every being stands for us.[114]

As the necessary condition for truth as correct correspondence, unconcealment should be regarded as the real essence of truth.

Unconcealment is Heidegger's more literal translation of the Greek word 'alētheia', usually just translated as truth. The word change itself is not the point; we 'get beyond an interchange of names' only if we 'come to know what must have happened in order to be compelled to say the *essence* of truth in the word "unconcealment"'.[115] The destruction of the tradition aims at revealing the phenomena that inspired the word or concept in the first place but has been subsequently covered up (see 65–6).

Now that we have a better grasp of Heidegger's understanding of truth, we can move to our second question: how is art a 'happening' of this truth? Representational artworks obviously show or unconceal things by depicting them, the way Van Gogh's painting portrays a pair of shoes. However, non-artworks represent too; a holiday snapshot apparently reveals the kids shaking hands with Mickey Mouse as much as Velasquez's 'Las Meninas' shows Infanta Margarita with her maids of honour.

Heidegger discerns two ways in which artistic representations are distinctive. First, as discussed above, artworks manifest their subject's mode of Being, even when this is difficult as with equipment (161–2). Second, great works of art highlight particularly telling details that illuminate a whole world the way Van Gogh's depiction of the shoes evoke the peasant's entire life and circle of activities, how she understands herself and the world around her. It is not uncommon to speak of how art shows us a world, i.e., the subject's *Weltanschauung*, what it is like to be this person or to live in their world. *Moby Dick* lets us experience the texture of a nineteenth-century whaler's life; *Sense and Sensibility* evokes what being an upper-class British woman in the late eighteenth century meant and felt like. Heidegger tries to capture this quality in his lyrical description of the peasant's world in Van Gogh's painting, her daily activities and her deepest concerns, brought out by a depiction of her shoes that bear the traces of her livelihood and the defining milestones of a life – birth, sustenance, celebration, need, death (159). The portrait of a humble but essential part of her world distills this complex and nuanced sense into a single item. Art can reveal an entire personality in a single action, expression, or possession; think of Hamlet's indecisiveness or Mona Lisa's smile. Attentively dwelling with such a work is like 'walking a mile in her shoes'.[116]

So far we have focused on how artworks illuminate particular beings, showing both their mode of Being and the world they help make up. Van Gogh's painting reveals much more of these than, say, a catalog photograph of a pair of shoes. But artworks 'do not simply make manifest what these isolated beings as such are . . . rather, they make unconcealment as such happen in regard to beings as a whole' (181). This claim surpasses anything we have discussed so far. Heidegger now moves from art's manifestation of beings to its revelation of Being itself, the fundamental fact that beings are present to us at all, that we are open to the world in various ways. As we saw, art can reveal equipmentality which is inconspicuous and thus difficult to grasp explicitly. Being, however, is what is most inconspicuous of all, so much so that we usually dwell in forgetfulness, oblivion, or unawareness. In terms reminiscent of equipment, Heidegger often says that 'as it reveals itself in beings, Being withdraws'.[117] Being is spelled out here in terms of the clearing or unconcealment of beings which 'grants and guarantees to us humans a passage to those beings that we ourselves are not and access to the being that we ourselves are'.[118]

We almost never notice this most basic of all facts – that we are aware at all – which Heidegger calls standing in the clearing. This is not because it is abstruse or complex but because it is so simple.[119] We 'keep to what is present without considering presencing' (EGT 99), that is, we focus on the items in front of us rather than on the fact that they *are* or that we can encounter them. This is natural and even inevitable most of the time; our daily activities would grind to a halt if we were continuously focusing on our openness.

> In order to bring into view what resides in a visual field, the visual field itself must precisely light up first, so that it might illuminate what resides within it; however, it cannot and may not be seen explicitly. The field of view, ἀλήθεια [*alētheia*], *must* in a certain sense be overlooked.[120]

Heidegger often cryptically says that unconcealment itself is concealed in favour of the unconcealed, but this just means that we pay attention to the entities that are unconcealed rather than the fact that they are present to us, i.e., unconcealment. Extending the idea from 'On The Essence of Truth' that truth belongs together with untruth (128), he says, 'the clearing in which beings stand is in itself at the same time concealment' (178) so that 'truth, in its essence, is un-truth'.[121] The revelation of a being conceals or draws our attention away from the astonishing simple fact that it is revealed; we miss Being for the beings.

A work of art, however, highlights this neglected 'layer' in three different ways. First, by vividly showing us a particular world such as that of Van Gogh's peasant, it draws our attention to the fact that we are in a world which orients us in a particular way or, as Heidegger sometimes puts it, that the world worlds. The world is not identical with the clearing as a whole (see 180), but represents the large 'sub-region' where we are at home and know our way around. The world is the meaningful context within which what we encounter makes sense.[122]

Like the clearing, the world usually recedes inconspicuously, directing our attention to the foregrounded entity: *'ordinary understanding cannot see the world for beings*, the world in which it must constantly maintain itself simply . . . to be able to pick out this or that being.'[123] Great artworks however make a world shimmer into visibility through particularly significant details, the way the peasant's shoes illuminate how things in general are for her. Evoking an entire world from the usually unnoticed bits and pieces of our daily lives, all artworks ultimately say the same thing: 'at bottom, the ordinary is not ordinary; it is extraordinary.'[124]

The second way that artworks effect this kind of truth returns us to the essay's starting point of the artwork's thingly element. To recap: the initial strategy guiding the first section was to understand art through its thingly aspect (145). This element initially struck us as the work's matter (152), but the form/matter scheme belongs to equipment (154). Using Van Gogh's painting of a piece of equipment, the work suddenly blossomed into a rich revelation of the peasant's world and of equipmentality as the shoes' mode of Being, incidentally uncovering the essence of art as setting up the truth of beings (162). We learned the methodological lesson that one category should not be explained in terms of another, that each region of beings deserves its own set of concepts and terms. This is the task Heidegger now takes up: to comprehend the fact that artworks are made out of something but in a 'wholly distinct way' (165), rather than by way of things or equipment.

As discussed above, equipment inconspicuously withdraws from our awareness as we focus on the goal we are pursuing. Heidegger now adds that tools are *designed* to let their material get absorbed into the task: 'the material is all the better and more suitable the less it resists vanishing' (171). If the hammer's material is appropriate in that it enables the tool to work properly, we will not think about it at all. Material only calls attention to itself when it fails; the wood or metal shows up as too light or too fragile.

The complete opposite is true of artworks' relation to what they are made of, as shown by the temple. 'By contrast the temple-work, in setting up a world, does not cause the material to disappear, but rather causes it to come forth for the very first time' (171). Whereas equipment only calls attention to its material when it fails, a work of art accomplishes this precisely when it succeeds. After the attempt to understand artworks in terms of form and matter failed, he now creates a new horizon specifically for artworks within which this element is called earth (194).

Earth is defined in opposition to, but also in necessary relation to, world (174). World is described in terms of opening and intelligibility (with phrases like measure, distinctive shape, scope, and limits), whereas earth is closing, concealing, and inexplicable. Paradoxically, earth virtually gets defined as the indefinable, that which resists getting fixed within a system of significance, i.e., a world. For instance, we can measure a stone's weight and explain it in terms of gravitational pull, and yet this determination somehow covers over or misses the immediate experience of heaviness, how it feels pressing down on our hand. In revealing meaningful features, such explanations of brute facts of the world simultaneously conceal our more immediate contact with things. Definitions dissolve raw 'qualia' in favour of concepts. Ultimately, heat 'is' just motion because it can be scientifically reduced to this, but the experience of hotness is fundamentally different from movement. To understand the stone in scientific terms is precisely to lose our raw experience of the heavy stony rock; the 'feel' or 'look' of a colour, its 'greenness', evaporates when considered as a wavelength. These kinds of explanations correlate a phenomenon with terms and ideas alien to its integral character, thus diluting or entirely eclipsing what it is like. Earth 'causes every merely calculating importunity upon it to turn into a destruction'.[125] One reason Heidegger uses tautologous phrases such as 'the world worlds' or 'the thing things' is to point to a phenomenon in its specificity without explanations or descriptions thinning it out.[126]

Of course, the trap here is that just calling something mysterious partially locates and defines it, thus destroying any radical mysteriousness.[127] Filing a phenomenon under the category 'mysterious' or 'incomprehensible' gives it a place within our comprehensive grasp. What is extraordinary about art is that it allows earth to present itself without integrating it into the world at all.

> This setting forth of the earth is achieved by the work as it sets itself back into the earth . . .. The sculptor uses stone just as the mason uses it, in his own way. But he does not use it up . . .. The painter also uses pigment, but in such a way that color is not used up but rather only now comes to shine forth.[128]

Representational art (to stay with this type of art for the moment) sets up a world by depicting something, but it accomplishes this through and in the medium of inherently nonrepresentational stuff: stone, pigment, sound tones, etc. Properly functioning equipment distracts us from its material, letting us make our way through the world with little to no thought. Great art on the other hand keeps us constantly aware of the fact that it is made of something, that the sculpture does not just represent a waking slave but represents him in *stone*. Whereas a (non-artistic) photograph withdraws as a 'magic window' through which we look at its subject, 'the work sets itself back into' (171) the material, keeping it within our attention. Let's look at this in a particular work.

Van Gogh's 'Starry Night' sets up a world by depicting a scene: a small village sleeps beneath a roiling night sky. We can look 'through' the painting to what it depicts, namely, the villagers' world – their daily routines, emotional lives, spiritual state, etc. The painting can, however, undergo a Gestalt switch into a piece of fabric with thick globs of paint on it, which would be earth. The two aspects can also switch back and forth, vying for dominance, which Heidegger calls strife. 'The world, in resting upon the earth, strives to surmount it. As self-opening it cannot endure anything closed. The earth, however, as sheltering and concealing, tends always to draw the world into itself and keep it there' (174). The magic window leads the eye to look through it, but the paint wants to be acknowledged, especially when one stands before the original; up close it dissolves into a splash of colours, breaking the illusion. A great representational work of art for Heidegger is one that creates a strife between what is depicted and the medium used to depict it, allowing us to see both. The tension between them makes us more vividly aware of each than in our mundane dealings with worldly equipment or earthy things: 'in essential strife ... the opponents raise each other into the self-assertion of their essential natures' (174). Bad art lets one thrive at the expense of the other, like potboiler novels which so absorb the reader into their world that she forgets that she is sitting on a couch running her eyes over squiggles of ink on paper, or overly experimental works that repel any attempts to enter them. In great art each makes the other stronger, as in Van Gogh's painting which vibrates with energy due to the beauty of the scene contrasting with the visible brush strokes.

By troubling the medium through which we perceive the subject, by disturbing the representational illusion, strife draws our attention to art's miraculous evocation of something deep and powerful in a splattering of paint or a chunk of rock. My awareness of my emotional state listening to Bach's Cello Suites is heightened when I realize that my rapture, my sense of profound insight, comes from rubbing horse hair across cat-gut bound to glued-together wooden boards. I cannot escape the feeling that such works express something profound about what it means to be human, yet they are 'really' just vibrations produced by rubbing strings together. This incongruity between the profound stirrings in my heart and their mundane cause, between art's meaningfulness and its medium's meaninglessness, makes me aware of music as music, which helps me feel gratitude for what I had been taking for granted. I am grateful that I can hear and, by extension, that I am in the clearing at all.

Since works make us aware of being aware, or unconceal the normally inconspicuous unconcealment, 'only now, in the midst of beings, the open region brings beings to shine and ring out'.[129] We are always within the clearing but we usually take it so much for granted that we are not aware of it. The 'friction' or resistance set up by strife prevents the clearing from inconspicuously withdrawing, thus allowing the truth or unconcealment of Being to take place: 'self-concealing Being is cleared' (181).

The third way that truth happens in art is through what Heidegger calls its 'createdness'. Although equipment is made, this only occurs to us when inappropriate material causes a malfunction: 'who was the idiot who made a hammer out of balsa wood and pewter?' On the other hand, 'in the work, createdness is expressly created into the created being, so that it stands out from it' (189–90). In strife, artworks set their subject back into what they are made out of, which constantly confronts us with the fact that meaning and emotional resonance have been wrought from mere stuff.

Ultimately, createdness makes us thematically aware of the fact that the artwork is, a fact that usually lies dormant or concealed in our dealings with beings. 'The simple *factum est* is to be held forth into the open region by the work: namely this, that unconcealment of a being has happened here . . . or, that such a work *is* at all rather than is not' (190). Artworks are, we might say, intentionally obtrusive; they do not go quietly into inconspicuousness but demand our attention as beings that are. This is totally different from equipment's createdness which 'does not become prominent in the equipment; it disappears in usefulness. The more handy a piece of equipment is, the more inconspicuous it remains that, for example, this particular hammer is.'[130] Equipment inconspicuously hides its 'that it is', which is why 'the making of equipment never directly effects the happening of truth' (189). Using tools dims down our awareness, lulling us into unthinking auto-pilot, whereas artworks 'restrain all usual doing and prizing, knowing and looking, in order to stay within the truth that is happening in the work' (191).

'What Is Metaphysics?' describes how the contingency of all beings, i.e., the recognition that they might not have been, highlights the simple fact that they are (103). Here, the artwork's strife keeps us aware that it has been created and thus that it is: seeing the earth of its world, e.g., the swirls of paint that make up the landscape, vividly exposes the fact that the artwork has come into being while it could have remained mere blobs of paint in tubes. The contingency of its existence brings its *factum est* to the forefront which imparts a sense of Being itself (190).

These three ways that artworks illuminate Being – setting up a world, instigating strife, and highlighting their own createdness – justify Heidegger's claim that the essay is completely oriented to the question of Being.[131] Like Dasein in *Being and Time* (see 55–6), artworks are privileged objects of inquiry since they have a special connection to Being that can help us achieve a proper relationship. One indication of this is how much time Heidegger spends analysing poetry in his later works.

Heidegger admits that organizing his discussion of art around truth is unusual since beauty has traditionally been the dominant topic of aesthetics (162). He does not neglect beauty, but joins it to truth in art. Truth is unconcealment and beauty is the unconcealment of this unconcealment which occurs in an exceptional way in great works of art. 'That is how self-concealing Being is cleared. Light of this kind joins its shining to and into the work. This shining, joined in the work, is the beautiful. *Beauty is one way in which truth essentially occurs as unconcealment.*'[132]

Although the clearing is usually 'self-concealing' in that it recedes while revealing beings, artworks provoke its revelation, revealing unconcealment itself, which is how Heidegger defines beauty. Being, truth, and beauty, three traditional values of philosophy, are innovatively joined together here.

In addition to truth and Being, Heidegger also places the good within art's realm. We can see this quasi-ethical aspect best when we turn from representational art, which we have concentrated on so far, to his deliberate selection of a Greek temple as a non-representational work (167). Instead of invoking a world by depicting a telling detail the way Van Gogh's portrait of the dirt-stained shoes does, the temple directly sets up the world of the Greeks: 'the temple, in its standing there, first gives to things their look and to men their outlook on themselves' (168). The temple manifests the Greek sense of what is important and what things mean, i.e., their epoch's understanding of Being.

As all worlds do, 'this open relational context' (167) provides 'a guiding measure, a form in which what is essential gives guidance' (169). Like the peasant's world, the temple 'first fits together and at the same time gathers around itself the unity of those paths and relations in which birth and death, disaster and blessing, victory and disgrace, endurance and decline acquire the shape of destiny for human being'.[133] The temple gathers the major landmarks that shape a human life into a meaningful pattern. Religion sanctifies; it takes up the brute facts of human life we are thrown into – birth, death, companionship, family, meals – and infuses them with meaning. The birth of my child is a biological act performed by my species, but a *Bris* or baptism joins my children to my wife and me, our past to our future, our family to our community. This kind of 'transubstantiation' or 'change-over' is how such events 'acquire the shape of destiny', how they become sacred. Rituals attune an entire community to see, think, and value in harmony as long as 'the god has not fled' (168), i.e., as long as this common understanding sufficiently suffuses the community's life.[134]

This infusion of meaning into our facticity applies the strife between earth and world to our lives. Earth in this case represents the brute facts that characterize humans – that we are born, eat, mate, die. Although these elements possess no intrinsic meaning, the rites and celebrations of a religion weave them into a pattern, or world, that turns birth into a gift, mating into the joining of souls, and death into a passage (see 362). Through celebrations, they become the meaningful inheritance of a people rather than the biological occurrences of a species.

Like bad artworks, religions compromise this strife when either earth or world overpower the other. World-dominance results from overly comprehensive or smug explanations, a complacent confidence that one possesses the only true religion and that everything happens for a reason, like Kierkegaard's despised Christendom. Sartrean nihilism, denying all meaning to the world in favour of the grey featurelessness that confronts us in anxiety, would be an excess of earth. Genuine strife acknowledges that our rituals do give life-events meaning without losing sight of their givenness or arbitrariness. *Ultimately*, circumcision is no more rational or correct than baptism or tattooing or any of a myriad of other ways to celebrate birth; had I been born another time or place I would undoubtedly believe in and live by a wholly different faith. But, because of the contingent facts of my background, it *does* hold meaning for me; it connects me to my son and both of us to millennia of ancestors and future generations. Although this bond is rationally indefensible, affiliation with tradition provides a way to be at home in this life and on this earth (see PR 15). I think this is what Heidegger means by 'the protective grace of the gods' (170).

I project the culture I have been thrown into by deliberately embracing and celebrating it. Of all that I am thrown into, of course, the most basic possible feature is simply being in a clearing at all. The 'ethical' prescription in much of Heidegger's later work is to project this most fundamental feature of our thrownness. 'The opening up of the open region, and the clearing of beings, happens only when the openness that makes its advent in thrownness is projected' (196). We most completely realize the clearing when we celebrate it, cherish and guard it. We ought to gratefully attend to the fact that we are open to beings, which art does exceptionally well. Listening to music helps us celebrate the simple fact that we can hear, painting that we can see, etc. Projecting openness itself, the fact that we have these ways of being open, is the foundation and culmination of particular celebrations.[135]

STUDY QUESTIONS

1 Explain world and earth and their strife. Describe how the strife occurs in a specific work of art.
2 How does strife occur in non-representational works, such as the temple?
3 Why did Heidegger create so many new terms?

d. Letter on Humanism

'Letter on Humanism' discusses many issues central to Heidegger's later career and is widely considered one of his most important writings. The essay as a whole, however, often appears to meander without purpose or structure. Whereas an essay like 'On the Essence of Truth' follows a clear (if dense) line of argument, it is much harder to see how the various discussions in 'Letter on Humanism' come together to form a coherent whole.

The obvious way to approach the essay is through the titular topic of humanism. Sartre had recently given a talk, later published as 'Existentialism Is a Humanism', rejecting the popular image of existentialism as pessimistically focused on despair and human weakness. Existentialism is actually the most hopeful school of thought, Sartre argues, since it maintains that what we are is entirely up to us. His famous claim that existence precedes essence means that we are not defined by a pre-existing Form or divinely given essence; we simply show up, radically free, and our subsequent decisions determine our essence. The death of God leaves us in 'a situation where there are only human beings' (quoted at 237), making us masters of our own fate and the source of the world's meaning and value.

In his talk, Sartre names Heidegger as a fellow atheistic existentialist. Whether or not we accept this assessment of the early work, Heidegger had come a long way in the twenty years since *Being and Time*. In particular, he spent the late-thirties studying Nietzsche's thought in great detail, concluding that his ideas (adopted and celebrated by Sartre as true humanism) are actually symptoms of our catastrophic era. This kind of humanism issues from and reinforces contemporary 'homeless-ness' which 'Nietzsche was the last to experience' (241). When Jean Beaufret poses questions about Sartre's talk, Heidegger seizes the opportunity to separate himself from Sartre by diagnosing this view.

Beaufret asks how we can restore meaning to 'humanism', to which Heidegger responds that the question assumes that such a goal is desirable (219, 247). Before we know whether or not we want to revive it, we must first investigate what humanism is, which he defines as helping humans become what they are.[136] This goal obviously assumes that there *is* something that humans are, that we possess what is traditionally called an essence.[137]

Sartre equates existentialism with humanism, but the latter's presupposition of an essence to humanity conflicts with the former's denial thereof. Heidegger admits that *Being and Time*'s claim that 'the "essence" of Dasein lies in its existence'[138] could be read the way Sartre does, but he wants to show that this is a misreading. Existence here names the articulated structure of Dasein's way of Being, not just what happens in a person's life (which is closer to the traditional notion of *existentia* or *actualitas*). Instead of asserting the mere fact that 'we live, "the sentence Man ek-sists". . . responds to the question concerning man's "essence"'.[139] The set of existentialia or essential structures that make up Dasein's existence functions in many ways like a traditional essence (see 59).

As a formal exhortation to be true to your nature, the meaning of humanism depends entirely on its view of human nature and our relations to beings as a whole, which have varied wildly throughout history. A civilized Roman citizen gets defined in terms of how he relates to barbarians, his family, and the city; seeing man as a child of God rests on an understanding of God and this fallen world; Marx's *homo faber* (producing or working man) gets its content from how he relates to natural needs, labour, and the social distribution of goods. Even Sartre explicitly bases his humanism on his ontology of godless reality. Such far-reaching conclusions about the nature of man and the purpose of life imply and follow from a particular conception of what it means to be (225). This leads to Heidegger's first major point: 'every humanism remains metaphysical'[140] by forming their views about man's essence on the basis of a conception of what it means to be, or metaphysics.

One's definition of the Being of beings dictates what one takes man's essence to be, which in turn determines that specific form of humanism. Let us briefly look at Christian humanism as an example.[141] For Christianity, to be is to be a creation of God, so everything gets its significance from His Ideas. History becomes fate, the divinely-authored story that passes from 'in the beginning' to the final judgment. We should strive to get as close to God as possible since He is the ground of all beings and the highest Being. The ontological break between heavenly things and the insurmountably inferior things of this world should guide all of our decisions. In this way, a particular meaning of Being and a specific understanding of how all beings relate to each other establishes this humanism.

Now Heidegger argues that this kind of thinking not only *misses* something vital, but actually blocks our access to it.[142] The ontological difference between beings and their Being guides the metaphysical quest to determine the Being of beings rather than gathering facts about individual beings.[143] However, metaphysics misses the truth of Being which lies beyond the ontological difference. Heidegger understands truth as unconcealment, i.e., the manifestation or presencing of beings to us in what he calls the clearing. Although metaphysics analyzes what beings are, it does not think about the simple fact that they are present to us at all. Indeed, Heidegger frequently says that it is its very simplicity that makes it hard to notice.[144] We tend to deal with beings without noticing that they are or that we are aware of them, 'forgetting the truth of Being in favour of the pressing throng of beings'.[145]

Heidegger mentions two ways that metaphysics has obscured the truth of Being: Plato explains the clearing with his theory of Ideas as the way beings 'look', while Kant (and Husserl) attribute beings' openness to our own transcendental faculties. Both commit the error of ontotheology by trying to explain Being itself in terms of beings.[146] These metaphysical examinations of beings as a whole and their Being prevent any inquiry into the truth or unconcealment of Being.[147] Instead of focusing on present things, this inquiry would turn to the highly elusive phenomenon of their presencing to us. We could not think about beings at all unless they manifested themselves to us, yet we do not think about this manifestation, or the truth of Being, itself. This is why Heidegger often says that Being withdraws or conceals itself in unconcealing beings. Focusing on what is lit up naturally ignores the light, presenting a kind of Gestalt switch between 'the presence of what is present and . . . what is present itself'.[148] Turning to this inconspicuous aspect requires a profound change in focus: rather than the nearest (particular beings), Heidegger is pointing to near*ness*, their presence to us, which is not at all another being.[149]

Heidegger draws another consequence from this refocusing that upends much of Sartre's thought, as well as Nietzsche's, and it has to do with the essay's very first sentence: 'we are still far from pondering the essence of action decisively enough' (217). Since he says a few sentences later that thinking is an action, this entails that we do not properly understand thinking either (see also 374). Whereas Sartre and Nietzsche (and to a lesser degree *Being and Time*) extend Kant's Copernican Revolution to depict consciousness as actively constituting the world and imbuing it with value, Heidegger's later work consistently emphasizes our passivity.[150] While our openness is who we are, it is not and cannot be of our doing; 'thinking accomplishes the relation of Being to the essence of man. It does not make or cause the relation. Thinking brings this relation to Being solely as something handed over to it from Being' (217). Our thinking can only be the recipient of our awareness of the world, not its source.

Being and Time explores this topic in the notion of thrownness: 'Dasein is something that has been thrown; it has been brought into its "there", but *not* of its own accord.'[151] Among all the particular features we discover ourselves possessing without having chosen them – our gender, race, etc. – our essential residence in the clearing or openness to Being is the first and the most fundamental, since everything else depends on this. 'We receive many gifts, of many kinds. But the highest and really most lasting gift given to us is always our essential nature, with which we are gifted in such a way that we are what we are only through it . . .. But the thing given to us, in the sense of this dowry, is thinking.'[152] The ability to think or to be aware of beings in any way is 'given' to us by Being. Of course, Being is not a being so this does not mean that the great Being in the sky sent us this gift like Prometheus handing fire to humanity or Michelangelo's God touching Adam with the spark of life (which would be an ontotheological account). What Heidegger means is that we can only find that beings reveal themselves to us. We cannot produce this unconcealment, since even to consider doing this requires us to know that there are things out there to be unconcealed, which means that they are already unconcealed to us in some way (this argument also appears in 'The Question Concerning Technology'). This ineliminable moment of passivity must form the basis for any kind of activity we engage in: 'how could man comport himself to beings – that is, experience beings as being – if the relationship to Being were not granted him?'[153]

The Greek notions of *alētheia* (usually translated as 'truth') and *physis* (roughly, the empirical realm of changeable things around us) capture the idea that Being reveals itself to us fairly well. Medieval thought credits a particular being – God – with opening the clearing, thus committing ontotheology, but at least the notion of a higher benefactor can provoke grateful awe. Heidegger sees the history of modern philosophy as the rise of subjectivity, which means that we take credit for opening the clearing and determining its character ourselves. Descartes sets this trend in motion by putting the subject at the forefront of philosophy and by claiming to construct a new more effective way of thinking. Kant then attributes the structure of the phenomenal world to transcendental subjectivity's unconscious activity, and Nietzsche brings this arc to its culmination by placing the conscious creation of values (and ontological structures) in the hands of the strong. The end result is that our era sees Being as what has been posited by subjects.[154]

We today, and many generations before us, have long forgotten the realm of the unconcealment of beings, although we continually take it for granted. We actually think that a being becomes accessible when an 'I' as subject represents an object. As if the open region within whose openness something is made accessible *as* object *for* a subject, and accessibility itself . . . did not already have to reign here as well![155]

Modern subjectivity claims responsibility for both the fact and the way that beings present themselves to us or, in Heidegger's terminology, the clearing.

Heidegger admits that *Being and Time* falls into this trap, or at least that it can be read that way. Its phrasing

> makes it all too possible to understand the 'project' as a human performance. Accordingly, project is then only taken to be a structure of subjectivity – which is how Sartre takes it, by basing himself on Descartes (for whom [*alētheia*] as [*alētheia*] does not arise). In order to counter this mistaken conception and to retain the meaning of 'project' as it is to be taken (that of the opening disclosure), the thinking after *Being and Time* replaced the expression 'meaning of being' with 'truth of being'.[156]

Sartre reads *Being and Time* as claiming that subjects supply all organization and value to an inert, absurd world, which is why he sees Heidegger as an ally. 'Letter on Humanism' aims to correct this misunderstanding of projection as 'an achievement of subjectivity' (231).

One way Heidegger makes this point is by emphasizing thrownness over projection. Whereas *Being and Time* awards a limited but important priority to projection, the later work shows thrownness inescapably dominating projection. What we decide to do depends on the options and preferences we are thrown into. 'All projection – and consequently, even all of man's "creative" activity – is *thrown*, i.e., it is determined by the dependency of Dasein on the being already in the totality, a dependency over which Dasein itself does not have control.'[157] The idea that Dasein projects a meaning of Being sounds too subjective, which is why Heidegger now says that 'man is rather "thrown" from Being itself into the truth of Being'.[158] In contrast to Sartre's picture of just humans, 'we are precisely in a situation where principally there is Being' (237).

Sartre frames the basic tenet of his talk in terms of two notions that have been central to philosophy since Plato (232) – essence and existence. Traditionally, a thing's essence precedes its existence in the sense that its Form or divine Idea guides its creation and determines what is proper to it. Knowing what a bed is and what it is for enables the craftsperson to make one, and knowing what we want it to do enables her to evaluate how well it serves its purpose, i.e., how good a bed it is. Sartre's innovation is to reverse this relationship so that for humans, existence precedes essence. We have no pre-set essence laying out what we are supposed to do; we create our essence during our existence through the radically free choices we make. But for Heidegger, 'the reversal of a metaphysical statement remains a metaphysical statement. With it [Sartre] stays with metaphysics in oblivion of the truth of Being.'[159] Just moving metaphysical terms around, no matter how creatively, cannot escape or seriously alter traditional ideas.[160]

Instead of assuming the validity of these standard ideas and just putting them into a novel arrangement, Heidegger takes a step back to challenge the notions themselves. 'The differentiation of *essential* (essentiality) and *existential* (actuality) completely dominates the destiny of Western history', but 'it still remains to ask first of all from what destiny of Being this differentiation . . . comes to appear to thinking'.[161] Throughout his career, Heidegger believes that humans tend to take their present situation for granted, as if their views were self-evidently correct. In the early work, this takes the form of Dasein's conformity to the one (*das Man*).

The later work casts this idea in historical terms. We generally take the way things are now as their natural state: 'it simply no longer occurs to us that everything that we have all known for so long, and all too well, could be otherwise.'[162] This complacency finds support in the standard conception of truth as a static correspondence with things as they are or, in Heidegger's terms, forgetting the truth of Being to focus on the state of beings.[163] The truth of Being is a dynamic event of unconcealment in which beings manifest themselves to be perceived, thought about, and acted on. As the 'irruption' (95) of beings out of concealment rather than the state of just being there, our experience loses its air of inevitability; as something that happens, it could happen other ways. Studying metaphysical writings from earlier ages shows how differently beings have presented themselves throughout history. While people in each era find their understanding self-evident, none of these ways of grasping reality can claim absolute validity; experience can fit each. Our own understanding is shown to be just one possible conception, not The Way Things Are. In this way, we move from uncritically engaging in metaphysical thinking to thinking about metaphysics from the perspective of the truth of Being.[164] Since it studies metaphysics from a higher or deeper point of view, this inquiry can be called '*meta-metaphysics*'.[165]

The fact that beings show up for us is not of our doing, and the same applies to how they show up: 'man does not decide whether and how beings appear' (234). How we think about the world depends on how it strikes us, what makes sense to us to say about it, none of which can be determined by us. In order to construct our way of thinking, we would need preferences and goals to guide the reform, and these could not be up to us on pain of infinite regress. Relevance, concepts, *that* something is so-and-so, are all phenomenological data that we simply find; we can only notice and think about 'what the addressed allows to radiate of itself'.[166] One of the leitmotifs of the later work is that thinking is essentially a response.

We are receptive in the fact that we can think at all, as well as the way we think. No matter what grounds we cite to justify our beliefs or procedures, down to accepting basic logical rules (such as the Principle of Reason or Non-Contradiction), it depends on our finding it authoritative, which itself cannot be finally grounded. Ultimately, we accept as sufficient and legitimate evidence that which strikes us as satisfactory.[167] Heidegger illustrates this by repeating the analysis of negation that appears in 'What Is Metaphysics?' (at 104–5), though it has special relevance here in light of Sartre's emphasis on the subject's production of negation. 'Every "no" that does not mistake itself as willful assertion of the positing power of subjectivity ... answers to the claim of the nihilation illumined' (260). We do not decide what can and should be negated; propositions present themselves to us as negatable.[168] The possibility of negating them must occur to us for us to consider doing it, and it must appeal to us as the right thing to do for us to choose to do it. We can formulate rules governing proper negation but, as Wittgenstein demonstrates, it is still up to us to determine when and how to apply them. Our action of negating is really a response to features presented to us rather than 'the product of a subjective act' (261).

According to this conception of thinking, how we think cannot be a matter of choice, nor can our most basic ways of thinking be justified since they are what determine what counts as justification in the first place. This is what Heidegger means by the phrase, 'groundless ground': although these ultimate notions form the foundation or ground for our thought, they themselves cannot be grounded.[169] This does not rob these laws of their legitimacy; indeed this is the only possible source of legitimacy.[170] Instead, it locates the laws within the wider context of the destiny of truth, that is, the various ways of thinking sent to us throughout history, including our present position as recipients of one particular epochal understanding of Being.

> In the beingness of beings, metaphysics thinks being, yet without being able to ponder the truth of being in the manner of its own thinking. Metaphysics everywhere moves in the realm of the truth of being, which truth, metaphysically speaking, remains its unknown and ungrounded ground . . .. It is necessary to ask what metaphysics is in its ground. This questioning must think metaphysically and at the same time think out of the ground of metaphysics.[171]

This project takes the philosophical drive to examine one's presuppositions to its conclusion by tracing the roots of our most basic ideas.

Now, we must keep in mind that the term 'groundless ground' has two sides: this 'measure' lacks ultimate justification, but it does supply us with ways of thinking that are as legitimate as they can be. In *Being and Time*, thrownness alluded to our existential abandonment in a strange realm; now Heidegger recasts this notion in a more positive light: 'man is rather "thrown" from Being itself into the truth of Being' (234). We are thrown into a way of thinking that can become a welcoming home where we dwell rather than an arid alien landscape. Our homelessness (*'Unheimlichkeit'*) is not a permanent feature of Dasein, but a contemporary historical symptom of our having forgotten Being (see 241–3). If it were really up to us to decide how to think and what to value without being attracted or repulsed by anything, as portrayed by the modern subject-centered philosophy like Sartre's notion of an original project, we would be paralysed, like Buridan's ass. Deciding for one way of thinking or living over another requires that I *find* one preferable to the other, that it attracts me. 'I cannot exist at all without constantly responding to this or that address in a thematic or unthematic way; otherwise I could not take so much as a single step, nor cast a glance at something.'[172] Whereas Nietzsche and Sartre's proposed solutions to nihilism demand that we create value through willed acts of valuing, Heidegger considers this the ultimate form of nihilism since it ignores the meaningfulness we find all around us.[173]

Heidegger uses the German phrase, '*Es gibt*' – generally translated as 'there is', but literally meaning 'it gives' – to bring out another point. Whenever 'there are' beings, they are 'given' to us in that the process of unconcealment is something that happens to us rather than something that we do. Again, we must resist the ontotheological image of a being supplying us with beings or forms of understanding. One reason Heidegger's writing is so difficult is that he is fighting against our language's propensity to speak only of beings, with no vocabulary or grammar to talk about Being (see 86). In this case, the tortured phrasing comes out as: 'the "gives" names the essence of Being that is giving, granting its truth. The self-giving into the open, along with the open region itself, is Being itself.'[174] Normally givers are distinct from their gifts and the act of giving, but in this case Being is not something alongside the given beings; it is the dynamic event of beings presenting themselves to us, as well as the 'space' or locale in which they become manifest. As difficult as it is to wrap your head around the idea, Being is the giving and the givenness of beings. In this way, 'it gives' resembles phrases like 'it is raining', where there is no separate agent doing the raining, no subsistent subject named by the 'it' (see WCT 172). The only 'thing' that is performing the action of raining is the rain itself which only exists in the act of raining; it is the agent, the act, and the stuff enacted all in one (this grammatical form is sometimes called the middle voice, between activity and passivity).

The subject-object grammar of our language also misleads us to think of ourselves as substantial entities[175] to which this event of appearing happens. Heidegger insists that we cannot properly think of ourselves or Being apart from the other: Being is essentially appearing which needs someone to appear to, and we are essentially involved with beings in their appearance to us.[176] Thus, whereas Sartre denies any essence to human consciousness, Heidegger assigns us a kind of essence, namely being open to Being. 'What man is – or, as it is called in the traditional language of metaphysics, the "essence" of man – lies in his ek-sistence.'[177] *Being and Time*'s term for our specific way of Being, existence, is now understood in light of its etymological roots in 'ec-stasis' or 'standing outside oneself', which means 'standing in the clearing of Being' (228) amongst beings rather than being closed up in some kind of inner mind.[178]

Now, Heidegger does not exactly call this an essence, but says that it takes the place of essence in the traditional sense. For one thing, it is far more dynamic: disclosing beings is closer to something that we do than a quality we have or state we are in. It is closer to the sense of Aristotele's *ergon*, or a being's distinctive activity. Also, the fact that Being gets revealed in radically different ways in different epochs renders the activity of revealing beings quite formal and flexible. Our essential openness is historical in that what kind of Being we reveal changes profoundly across epochs: 'man stands ek-sistingly in the destiny of Being. The ek-sistence of man is historical as such' (239). Heidegger rebukes both Sartre and Husserl for ignoring this point while praising Hegel for discovering it.[179]

This understanding of our 'essence' leads Heidegger to a new comprehension of ethics. Like most continental thinkers, Heidegger refuses to issue specific 'directives' or 'rules' for good living (255). Instead, he discusses ethics in the sense of its etymological origin, *ēthos*, meaning 'abode, dwelling place' (256). This means the place where we dwell which makes us what we are, thus pointing to the clearing.[180] This line of thought adapts a very old form of ethics, sometimes called perfectionism, which receives its canonical formulation in Aristotle's *Nicomachean Ethics*. The idea is that once we find our essence or what makes us distinctive (our *ergon*), the best way of living consists in performing this activity with excellence (*arête*). For Heidegger, our distinctive activity is ek-sistence or revealing Being: 'man is, and is man, insofar as he is the ek-sisting one' (252). This is basic to our doing anything else and, as far as we know, no other being can do this (an important criterion of distinctiveness in Aristotle's system).[181] Therefore, to be a good man means to reveal Being well, which is why thinking about the truth of Being is the original ethics.

We perform our activity with excellence by taking care of Being. Heidegger says many times that man is thrown into the clearing 'so that ek-sisting in this fashion he might guard the truth of Being'.[182] Whereas in *Being and Time* thrownness is fairly close to Sartre's claim that we are abandoned in the world with no essential task assigned to us by anything like nature or God (see BT 393/343), now Being throws us into a particular task, namely revealing Being. This activity has a highest form, which Heidegger variously calls being the shepherd of Being (234, 245) or, altering another term from *Being and Time*, caring for Being (231, 246, 390). The truth of Being 'thoroughly governs' (233) us in that we can only think and experience in terms of our epoch's particular understanding of Being. This holds for everyone but, in the oblivion of Being, we do not explicitly attend to it, leaving us unable 'to experience and take over this dwelling'.[183] A few thinkers and poets manage to bring their understanding to explicit awareness and articulation, the way phenomenology dredges up the structures of consciousness for thematic attention.[184]

The great thinkers and poets reach beyond the specific understanding of Being they live in to the bedrock level of having an understanding of Being at all, being open to anything whatsoever. Before the particulars of *what* is open to us, we should ponder the fact *that* Being is open to us in any way, that we dwell in openness, that there is Being (see 238). We find and raise to awareness that within us that corresponds to Being; Being is the appearance of beings and we are the appeared-to.[185]

A number of features characterize this excellent disclosure. The first is paying close, sensitive attention to how beings appear to us, allowing them to unfold their appearance the way one nurtures a plant to maturation. We should let beings be (*Gelassenheit*), let them fully manifest themselves as they 'want' to, rather than forcing them into presupposed concepts.[186] Since Being itself withdraws as it presents us with beings, we should allow Being itself to come into the open by contemplating the emergence of various forms of epochal beingness in the history of metaphysics. Perhaps the most important way to reveal Being well is to put it into language. Heidegger famously starts the essay with the idea that 'language is the house of Being . . .. Those who think and those who create with words . . . [accomplish] the manifestation of Being insofar as they bring the manifestation to language'.[187] Since our encounters with Being are inherently linguistic, bringing Being explicitly to language represents the fulfillment or 'accomplishment' (217) of our relationship.[188]

Throughout, we should celebrate our possibly unique ability to bring beings to manifestness. This is how Heidegger insists that his later work is a form of humanism, and a superior one to Sartre's which 'does not set the *humanitas* of man high enough' (233–4). Sartre claims that his system awards man the highest place by putting him in charge as the one who orders the world and creates values. Heidegger responds that this position is both incoherent (as discussed above) and leads to nihilism or the complete loss of value. Willfully choosing all values as in Sartre's fundamental project must reject any guidance as heteronomous alien interference; values that precede our decisions would weight us down with an essence. With no given preferences or criteria (since their significance can only be determined in light of our previously chosen fundamental project), the choice can only be arbitrary; as the foundation of all further values, this drains the entire structure of significance. As the Medieval rationalists objected to their voluntarist opponents, an absolutely undetermined choice of good and bad cannot be good in principle, since it is the source of all evaluation.

Heidegger argues that it is the necessarily passive reception of preferences and criteria that enables us to make choices at all. We receive 'from Being itself the assignment of those directives that must become law and rule for man . . .. Only such dispatching is capable of supporting and obligating. Otherwise all law remains merely something fabricated by human reason.'[189] Reversing Kantian autonomy,[190] Heidegger argues that only that which lies beyond us can obligate us. Acts of valuing that arise solely from our opting to value certain things can be changed or retracted at will; ultimately, they can only reflect the basic desire to have our own desires fulfilled or, as he often puts it, our will willing itself. Heidegger's rejection of such values is not nihilism, but the only way to overcome nihilism. Obligation, the sense of responsibility to something greater, can only come from a source external to us.

Playing on the sense of gift as something precious to be treasured, Heidegger wants us to gratefully acknowledge our reception of significance as a gift. We do this by bringing it into the clearing by thinking about it, which is why he likes the word-play that thinking (*Denken*) is thanking (*Danken*).[191] We are given the ability to think, and using it brings us, as well as the gift and giver (Being), to their highest form.[192] Since what we find when we do this is a world full of meaning, this thinking also overcomes our contemporary homelessness, showing us that we dwell in a home-like world (242–3). Thus, 'demoting' ourselves from the source of all values actually enhances our status. 'Man is not the lord of beings. Man is the shepherd of Being. Man loses nothing in this "less"; rather, he gains in that he attends the truth of Being' (245). Ironically, Sartre's humanism does not put man high enough. As Being's servant, charged with the sacred task of guarding its truth, Heidegger's Being-centered humanism actually places us higher.[193]

STUDY QUESTIONS

1   What does Heidegger find problematic about Sartre's claim that existence precedes essence?
2   How does Heidegger understand 'ethics'? How does his own thought fit this definition of ethics? How is his thought a humanism?
3   How does forgetting the truth of Being do so much damage, and how is recalling it supposed to help so much?

e. Modern Science, Metaphysics, and Mathematics

This is probably the most readable piece in the collection. The writing is straightforward with just a few of the convolutions and neologisms that populate Heidegger's other essays, and the ideas may strike many readers as rather familiar. Both Thomas Kuhn's philosophy of science[194] and Foucault's post-structuralist analyses of science (see Chapter 4) employ similar frameworks.

However, there are some interesting and subtle things going on here that are not immediately visible, and the work gives us a sense of Heidegger's thoughts on the history of thought, an important aspect of his work that is underrepresented in this anthology.

The selection here is an excerpt from *What Is a Thing?*, a 1935–36 lecture series on Kant. Heidegger views Kant as primarily interested in ontology rather than epistemology,[195] so that the first *Critique* explains what things must be like in order to yield to scientific analysis. Heidegger also links the investigation of what things are to an analysis of science. However, whereas Kant takes Newtonian physics as the sole scientific truth about reality, the final word that renders earlier systems obsolete, Heidegger spends this paper exploring 'the Characteristics of Modern Science in Contrast to Ancient and Medieval Science' (271). Thus, Heidegger moves from asking 'what is a thing' to asking 'how is modern science different from previous forms?' We need to understand why he explores these epochal sciences, and why an examination of the nature of things should detour through science at all. Why does he not, as the motto of phenomenology puts it, go to 'the things themselves' to find out what things are?

In fact, the main point Heidegger makes in this piece is that we do not and cannot immediately confront bare things or uninterpreted facts. Rather, as Kant argued, things always appear within a horizon or 'conceptual scheme' which guides our experience and treatment of them; facts are always already interpreted. In a straightforward formulation of this idea, he says that 'there are no mere facts, but . . . a fact is only what it is in the light of the fundamental conception'.[196] Facts only mean something within a particular interpretation or horizon, what Heidegger sometimes calls the Being of that being or the contemporary understanding of Being. Thus, the question 'what is a thing' points us towards the horizon within which we experience things, their 'thingness'. For Kant, things are phenomena which have been structured by our forms of intuition and concepts of the understanding into scientifically knowable objects (see WT 190). Although Heidegger's own work usually broadens this investigation to encompass non-scientific contexts,[197] he follows Kant's lead here in focusing on science as the gateway to thingness. Although an epoch's understanding of Being gets stated most explicitly in the period's metaphysics, this understanding determines all of the disciplines at that time and so should be visible in its science as well.[198]

I. SECTION A

This excerpt attempts to grasp the essence of modern science and its roots in modern metaphysics through its particular take on mathematics. It is always hard to perceive the horizon one currently inhabits,[199] so Heidegger decides to illuminate modernity's defining features by contrasting it with ancient Greek science.[200] Section A quickly runs through three features commonly used to distinguish the two:

1 Modern science is based on hard facts and observations whereas previous inquiry relies on free-floating speculation or mere 'concepts' (271–2).
2 Unlike the Greeks, modern science employs experiments to discover information and test hypotheses (272).
3 Modern science uses calculations and measurements, ignored by ancient science (273).

Although Heidegger challenges all three claims – arguing that each 'modern' method was actually present in ancient science – his larger point is that this whole way of comparing is misguided. Investigating whether or not different periods use the same techniques to study nature ignores the difficulty involved in identifying them as the same. Even if certain contemporary practices occurred in an earlier form of science, they functioned and were understood in a fundamentally different way. For example, on the issue of experiments (#2), it is not a matter of what activities they undertake so much as the way it was done and how they understood what they were doing, which ultimately get grounded in a certain 'kind of preconception about things' (272). Heidegger is arguing for a holistic understanding of science, in which individual features such as practices can only be understood against the background of an era's scientific endeavour as a whole. Transporting 'the same' feature to a different context profoundly alters it.

Therefore, we must turn from individual aspects to the background understanding that determines their meaning, i.e., the period's metaphysical horizon of the thingness of things that 'rules and determines the basic movement of science itself' (273). This strategy looks beneath superficial differences among an era's sciences to the fundamental core that motivates and unifies all of its aspects. Like Kuhn's paradigm, our conception of what it means to be determines how we investigate beings, what kinds of questions make sense to ask about them, and what kinds of answers will count as acceptable. Since individual results can be interpreted differently depending on one's general understanding, it is only at this metaphysical level that we can explain why science changes. The idea that 'modern science is *mathematical*' (273) gives us the clue that will lead us to this foundational level, but we must be careful – this is not mathematics in the sense of the study of numbers.

II. SECTION B

Having eschewed its normal definition, Heidegger begins the next section by trying to explain his sense of the mathematical (273). As is his wont, he traces the word back to its Greek roots, according to which, the *mathēmata* are the general features of a set of things that we are familiar with prior to experience with them: 'the animal-like of the animal, the thingness of the thing, and so on'.[201] The *mathēmata* are the general categories by which we recognize and understand individual beings, the horizons or regions of ontology that orient our interactions with things. Heidegger often argues that we need a horizon or understanding of Being in order to discern beings at all, as well as to interact appropriately with them, making the mathematical 'the fundamental presupposition of the knowledge of things' (278).

As what underlies and enables experience, these conceptual schemes cannot be derived from experience. Rather than a conclusion resulting from examinations of beings, 'the mathematical is that evident aspect of things within which we are always already moving and according to which we experience them as things at all, and as such things' (277). In order to acquire the concept 'tree' empirically, for instance, we would first need to pick out a set of trees and only trees in order to abstract their common features. But selecting such a group already requires a mastery of the category 'tree' in order to select only things of this type for study out of all the things in the world.[202] This is a version of Meno's paradox, meant to demonstrate the impossibility of answering Socrates' 'what is X' question. Plato's theory of recollection – the idea that we have a vague grasp of the Forms which enables us to recognize the right answer when we come across it – solves it. Heidegger's solution bears a striking resemblance to this idea.

Heidegger argues that we could not recognize or single out features to study without a previous familiarity with their concept. Numbers represent a clear example because objects in the world do not 'contain' or present mathematical (in the standard sense) qualities to plain perception. 'Rather, we can count three things only if we already know "three". In thus grasping the number three as such, we only expressly recognize something which, in some way, we already have' (276). Before we could even notice this facet of things – i.e., their countability – we must be open to it; we must have the capacity to have our attention caught by it in order to attend to it. If we lacked the concept of number, we would just experience chairs, apples, and cats, but never three of anything. This exemplary status is why the term 'mathematical' has become attached to the science of numbers according to Heidegger.

This notion of the mathematical links Plato's theory of recollection (mentioned at 290–1) with Kant's account of the transcendental subject's constitution of the phenomenal realm by means of a priori concepts and Heidegger's own early work on Dasein's pre-ontological understanding of Being.[203] Each defines learning as achieving a more explicit awareness of what we already know or is somehow within us in a less conscious manner, rather than the discovery of something entirely new or foreign. Platonic learning means remembering the Forms that the soul encountered prior to this life but forgot due to the trauma of birth and the distractions of the flesh. Kant views science as consciously retracing the organization that one's own mind has autonomically imparted to phenomena. And Heidegger's early phenomenological work articulates the structure of the experiences we have all the time but do not pay attention to.

III. SECTION C

Now that we have determined the mathematical as what underlies and motivates specific practices, we can construct a proper contrast between modern and ancient science from this perspective. Aristotle represents the zenith of ancient Greek science, while Newton will serve as the representative modern scientist. Newton's first Law of Motion, the principle of inertia, strikes us today as 'self-evident' (280), as little more than an articulation of what everyone sees simply by looking at moving things. Intuitions like this lead to 'Whiggish' histories of science that portray the Progress of Enlightenment whereby over time, people stopped clinging to presuppositions and superstitions to finally pay attention to what really happens.

Heidegger scoffs at this kind of narrative.[204] It was not that people before Newton were stupid or stubbornly refused to see what was right before their eyes. Rather, they saw something different due to their particular understanding. Earlier periods could not have discovered the law of inertia because they experienced reality in a fundamentally incompatible way; in Kuhn's famous phrase, 'the proponents of competing paradigms practice their trades in different worlds'.[205] Although we moderns find the idea of inertia obvious, 'during the preceding fifteen hundred years it was not only unknown, but nature and beings in general were experienced in such a way that it would have been senseless' (280).

A period's metaphysics structures its science, setting limits to allowable ideas and possibilities. Continuing his idea that every unconcealment is also a concealment,[206] Heidegger argues that the Greeks' understanding showed them the world in one way while simultaneously hiding other ways. It was not that they simply missed a key piece of evidence; their way of understanding Being cast all evidence into a form that could not accommodate an idea like inertia. For the Greeks, physical bodies are just not the kind of thing that can engage in inertial movement. In order to grasp not just *what* a period believes but *why* they held those beliefs, one must look beneath individual ideas to their foundational metaphysical system.

IV. SECTION D

Heidegger now lays out Aristotle and Newton's distinct conceptions of nature, which represent their respective answers to the question 'what is a thing'. Although both natural philosophers are deeply committed to empirical data, their divergent perspectives show them quite dissimilar evidence. 'For *what* is actually apprehended as appearing and *how* it is interpreted are not alike' (282–3).

Heidegger applies the earlier idea that facts are always interpreted (272) to the starting point for both physics: motion.

> It is everywhere a question of the motion of bodies. But how motion and bodies are to be conceived and what relation they have to each other is not established and not self-evident. From the general and indefinite experience that things change, come into existence and pass away, thus are in motion, it is a long way to an insight into the essence of motion and into the manner of its belonging to things (283).

Once again, a superficial similarity masks a profound and subtle incommensurability; although both thinkers start from the simple fact that things move, what each makes of this holistically depends on the system within which it is viewed. There is no such thing as motion in-itself which univocally dictates what we are to make of it. Our theories are 'underdetermined' by the data, meaning that various theories can accommodate 'the same' observations by interpreting them differently. Their varying understandings of Being or metaphysics determine what they make of motion, thus bridging the gap from observation to scientific analysis. The kind of being that belongs to things decides how their motion is to be understood.

Aristotle's universe contains absolute differentiations among bodies, motions, and places. The four sub-lunary elements or basic kinds of matter (earth, water, air, and fire) each have their own place: earth's place lies at the bottom while fire's domain is on top, and ether's superlunary place behaves differently from everything beneath it. These are absolute directions within a qualified, heterogeneous space: earth falls down and fire rises because each type of body seeks its proper place. This kind of motion is natural while motion which violates it, such as throwing a rock upwards or submerging a bucket full of air, is unnatural or violent and cannot long endure. Motion is not a force externally imposed upon inert matter but arises from things' inner nature, so the way a thing moves depends on the type of thing that is moving. This is Aristotle's mathematical, his projection of thingness which guides the features of his physics. Notice that Aristotle can cite plenty of evidence ('look at how rocks fall down while fire rises') and explain lots of phenomena ('a thrown rock will eventually fall because sideways motion through the air is unnatural to earth; it seeks its proper place beneath'). This is not superstitious myth-making or story-telling; it simply starts from different principles than contemporary science.

Heidegger then contrasts Aristotle's system with Newton's as representative of the modern epoch, focusing once again on motion. Newton's first law begins with 'every body', immediately obliterating 'the distinction between earthly and celestial bodies . . ... All natural bodies are essentially of the same kind' (286). Qualitative differences between parts of space have also been stripped off; the Cartesian grid in which points occupy neutral positions replaces Aristotle's graduated, place-filled universe. Newton's conception of thingness erases Aristotle's distinctions between elements, motions, regions, etc., making scientific laws truly universal (as Kant demands); the falling of an apple obeys the same laws as the rotation of galaxies. Heidegger's claim is that these laws can only function like this, indeed Newton could only find them sensible, on the basis of a deep commitment to the homogeneity of space and things. Since things are inert material laying about within the neutral container of space, they can have no preferences about where they are or what kind of motion they engage in.[207]

Whereas the initial distinction between ancient and modern science listed isolated differences (that were inaccurate to boot), Heidegger has now shown how 'all these changes are linked together and uniformly based on the new basic position expressed in the First Law and which we call mathematical' (288). This analysis fulfills his promise to find the unifying explanation for all the disparities between these periods' sciences in the fact that 'the concept of nature in general changes'.[208] Aristotle and Newton's conceptions of motion had to clash because they were based on conflicting understandings of what things are.

V. SECTION E

The law of inertia would have been nonsense to the Greeks since it does not fit into their coherent understanding of Being. As in Quine's web of belief, ideas and facts near the edge of the web can be altered with few ramifications, but overturning those near the center calls for the entire fabric to be rewoven, since they are intertwined with so many others. These ideas – the mathematical – are what interest Heidegger. New understandings of these facts mark epochal turns in what he calls '*actual history . . . that always concerns the openness of Being*'.[209] These scientific revolutions force scientists to rethink the basic guiding concepts of their discipline, turning from scientific inquiry to philosophical questions like 'what is reality', or 'what is time?'[210] Although the transition from Medieval to modern times spreads across a couple of centuries (279), Heidegger examines one telling moment in detail: when Galileo drops two objects of different weights from the tower of Pisa. This represents one of modernity's first examinations of motion by an experiment, one of the ways people often distinguish modern science from Medieval.

The modern universe is profoundly homogeneous: 'all bodies are alike. No motion is special. Every place is like every other' (291). The law of gravity therefore applies the same way to everything, so the two objects should fall at the same pace rather than the thing with more earth racing faster to its 'home'. The bodies did not actually hit the ground simultaneously, however, disconfirming Galileo's hypothesis. But instead of bowing to the experiment's results, Galileo made an *ad hoc* adjustment to compensate for the unexpected data. Although regarded as a hero of modern science, Galileo is the one ignoring 'plain' evidence while the Medieval spectators remain faithful to it.[211]

This point in history, right on the edge of a revolution, yields the peculiar phenomenon of people who live at the same time but in different epochs. They stand side-by-side looking at the 'same' data but through different understandings, so they see different things.

> Both Galileo and his opponents saw the same 'fact'. But they interpreted the same fact differently and made the same happening visible to themselves in different ways . . .. Both thought something along with the same appearance but they thought something different . . . fundamentally, regarding the essence of a body and the nature of its motion.[212]

This episode vividly demonstrates the way facts depend on their interpretation. Since Galileo's answer to the question 'what is a thing?' diverges from his contemporaries, he sees a different event and draws different inferences from it. This scenario functions roughly as a third argument against the possibility of an empirical derivation of the mathematical: since Galileo and the spectators came to contradictory conclusions from the same 'fact', facts themselves cannot determine their own interpretation.

The mathematical precedes experience and even counts, in a Kantian vein, as the condition for the possibility of certain kinds of experience: 'the project first opens a domain where things – i.e., facts – show themselves'.[213] This domain is a kind of clearing, the 'site' within which humans have access to beings, but one which determines how beings can show up. Instead of a neutral arena which allows anything to appear, these disciplinary domains are circumscribed and structured by a 'basic blueprint' (291) from which 'unfolds the entire realm of posing questions and experiments, establishing laws, and disclosing new regions of beings' (293). The modern domain only allows uniform things homogeneously obeying universal laws to appear; aberrant phenomena are 'puzzles' awaiting integration into this scheme. Moreover, this uniformity of things and relations is what 'makes possible and requires a universal uniform measure as an essential determinant of things, i.e., numerical measurement'.[214] Modern science is mathematical in the sense of admitting only quantifiable phenomena because of its specific mathematical in the sense of its determining preconceptions about reality or things. The various aspects of an epoch fit together to form that period's coherent mathematical. 'How [things] show themselves in prefigured in the project. Therefore, the project also determines the mode of taking in and studying what shows itself, experience.'[215]

VI. SECTION F

Although every epoch is mathematical in the sense of operating within a set of preconceptions, modern science takes an unprecedented stance towards its mathematical. Medieval thinkers find out about the world by consulting the authorities on the matter – ultimately, the Bible and Aristotle; any other sources stand in need of external justification and must cohere with the official dogma contained therein. The modern era begins by rejecting this reliance on divine revelation and authoritative texts for justification. Modern thought dispenses with external authority in order to achieve a self-reliant ground for truth and legitimacy. In contrast to Greek conformity to the *cosmos logos* or Christian obedience to God's will, modernity gives rise to 'a new experience and formation of freedom itself, i.e., a binding with obligations that are self-imposed . . .. The mathematical strives out of itself to establish its own essence as the ground of itself and thus of all knowledge'.[216] As in Kant's ethical autonomy, only laws that we impose upon ourselves can bind us.

This drive towards self-reliance becomes the clue to understanding the founder of modern philosophy, Descartes. As with Kant, Heidegger reads Descartes as primarily interested in metaphysics rather than epistemology; his ideas about knowledge are consequences of his understanding of Being and, in particular, of thingness. Descartes does not first decide to doubt which then uncovers the foundational ego; doubt is how he fulfills the modern mathematical's demand to found knowledge for oneself (301). It is not as much their dubiousness as the fact that his prior beliefs were 'pregiven' (301) to reason that requires their ejection until properly inspected. Only by purging these alien ideas can he achieve the goal of the mathematical: 'taking cognizance of that which we already have'.[217]

Descartes devises a method whereby we can control which beliefs we admit into our thinking, taking care to restock our minds only with true ones. Since these beliefs include what is real, this method sets up reason as 'guideline and court of appeal for all determinations of Being'.[218] We decide the criteria that anything must meet in order to be considered real. Instead of being open to however things show up, our project decides which appearances will count as legitimate and which must be dismissed. Only what fits in with one's axioms can be real and true. Mathematically measurable qualities and movements conform to his system and hence really characterize (material) thingness; qualities such as beauty or usefulness do not and hence get relegated to mere subjectivity.

Ultimately, the 'I' doing this thinking is what precedes everything given externally, making it the highest axiom and the arbiter of the real: 'the Being of beings is determined out of the 'I am' as the certainty of the positing' (302). Descartes discovers and secures the self before God because the thinking I takes the place of God as determining reality. This is how Heidegger understands the way Descartes changes the meanings of 'subject' and 'object'. Whereas 'subject' previously meant any subsistent entity, it now denotes the 'I' as 'the referential center of beings as such'.[219] Things become objects which no longer subsist on their own, but can only be what they are by presenting themselves to the subject. The German word '*Gegenstand*' suggests this view since it literally means 'to stand against', making it dependent on something against which to stand. For Heidegger, subjects make objects stand-against them by representing them, in harmony with the early modern 'idea idea'. Rather than beings emerging with their own nature (Greek) or receiving it as divine gift (Medieval), modern man determines reality's character.

Knowledge has always been based on a projection which determines the real and how we investigate it – i.e., the mathematical – but modern thinkers are the first to try to grasp and control their own mathematical. Descartes sets up rules to manage and direct reason in order to become the author of his own way of thinking. 'With the *cogito-sum*, reason now becomes *explicitly* posited according to its own demand as the first ground of all knowledge and the guideline of the determination of the things' (304, italics in original). The significant feature of modernity is less the content of our mathematical than the stance we take towards it. We want to create and control our way of thinking, which in turn determines reality, thus achieving complete autonomy. 'What is decisive is that man specifically takes up this position as one constituted by himself . . .. Man makes depend on himself the way he is to stand to beings as the objective'.[220]

This ambition predetermines the rest of modern philosophy; later thinkers simply unpack its implicit consequences or play variations on its theme.[221] Kant's transcendental subject who gives nature its 'order and regularity' and Nietzsche's *Übermensch* who creates her own values and organizes the chaos of reality are simply extensions of Descartes' project. Of course, this unity also means that if we can pull a thread or two loose – such as the definition of ourselves as subject or thinking as willful autonomy – the entire edifice of metaphysics could unravel.[222]

STUDY QUESTIONS

1 What lessons does Heidegger draw from Galileo's experiment?
2 What is the mathematical? What role does it play in science? Why can't it be empirically derived?
3 What is so distinctive about Descartes' thought? Is Heidegger right to view modern thought as monolithically unified?

f. The Question Concerning Technology

I have always found this to be one of Heidegger's best essays. Its combination of persuasive phenomenological descriptions with a powerful argument can be more easily applied to concrete experience than the abstract musings on Being that populate many of his later writings. In particular, this essay dovetails nicely with 'Letter on Humanism' and 'Modern Science, Metaphysics, and Mathematics' by treating many of the same ideas with greater concentration than the latter and greater clarity than the former. The three can be fruitfully read together.

I. TECHNOLOGY AND ITS ESSENCE

Heidegger opens by distinguishing between technology and the essence of technology, stating that the latter is not at all technological (311). This distinction is not as puzzling or perverse as it might initially sound. Just as the essence of a tree is not itself a tree, so the essence of technology is not itself a piece of technology. The consequences of this seemingly simple point ripple throughout the entire essay. What Heidegger means by technology is straightforward: machines that perform tasks with greater efficiency than human hands. Such machines are created by us to function as 'a means to an end' (312); we make them in order to accomplish tasks more easily. Heidegger considers this 'instrumental and anthropological definition' (312) to be correct but not true,[223] which means that while it does capture certain facts about technology, it does not dig deep enough. It takes technology for granted, without asking how it is possible. Technology is a consequence of the essence of technology and can only be understood in light of this essence.

In order to find the essence of technology, Heidegger goes through one of his chain-like series of ideas. Starting with the initial definition of technology as a man-made means, he finds that the notion of a means to an end is generally viewed as the cause of that end. In order to understand instrumentality, then, we must grasp causality, which leads to a discussion of Aristotle's doctrine of four causes (313). Like most traditional theories, this idea has rigidified into unquestioned dogma that seems to have 'fallen from heaven as a truth as clear as daylight' (314). Continuing his early project of a 'destruction' of the tradition,[224] Heidegger wants to break through this obviousness to see causality anew, leading him to ask questions like, why are there four causes, and why *these* four? Instead of taking the idea for granted, he is asking 'what does "cause" really mean' (314)? Like Socrates' response upon receiving a list of examples when he had requested a definition, Heidegger wants to know what makes these four causes *causes*.

He unifies the four by reference to a more sensitive appreciation of the Greek term '*aition*', initially used in courtrooms in the sense of responsibility for a crime. Causes are the inter-related factors that collectively bear responsibility for an entity existing or lying there before us (314). Were any missing, the entity would not be. Since for Heidegger to be is to come into appearance, 'the four ways of being responsible bring something into appearance' (316). The final link of the chain explains this coming to appearance as 'bringing-forth brings out of concealment into unconcealment' (317), thereby tying technology to his usual definition of truth as unconcealment. Connecting this conclusion back to the starting point, we find that 'technology is a way of revealing'.[225]

II. THE ESSENCE OF TECHNOLOGY AS A WAY OF REVEALING

Heidegger now pauses (marked by a break in the text) to review this chain of ideas, expressing surprise at the conceptual distance traveled from technology to revealing (318). Revealing turns out to be the condition for technology. In order for us to make something, the materials and the goal must be revealed to us;

we have to be aware of them in order to use them or, really, to interact with them in any way whatsoever. Technology, like every comportment towards beings, presupposes the clearing, that is, our ability to encounter and be aware of entities.

However, Heidegger means much more than this. Throughout his career, he insists on the hermeneutic principle that perception is always the perception of a meaningful being.[226] Everything we encounter appears as a specific *kind* of thing, with no bare observations of featureless beings.[227] Moreover, the categories or horizons within which we experience beings are historical in that every epoch has its own predominant interpretation of beings or way beings manifest themselves. Many of his later writings, including 'Modern Science, Metaphysics, and Mathematics' in this anthology, try to uncover these epochal understandings of Being. This essay gives a quasi-phenomenological description of the way things reveal themselves to us today, which he calls 'enframing' (*Ge-stell*). This way of appearing to us is what makes technology possible.

In order for us to put objects together to make a machine, it is not enough that we just perceive them; they must be manifest *as* parts, as entities suitable to this task, as 'put-togetherable-to-make' the machine, so to speak.[228] So too must the goal present itself to us as attainable and desirable for us to embark upon the project in the first place. The far shore beckoning as to-be-reached is what starts me building a ship and then, within the horizon of the project, wood announces itself as good building material. My act of construction rests upon a receptive perception of the goal along with the materials and tools to reach it. Any problem we choose to work on must show itself as ought-to-be-fixed-through-tools. If for instance our trials and tribulations appeared as divine punishment visited upon us to test our humble subservience, then they would call upon us to weather them patiently, condemning any attempt to fix them as hubris.

Although the discussion has so far focused on Greek craftwork, Heidegger is primarily interested in what is distinctive about modern technology. Certainly, 'it too is a revealing' (320), but it reveals reality as 'standing-reserve' (*Bestand*) according to which 'everywhere everything is ordered to stand by, to be immediately on hand, indeed to stand there just so that it may be on call for a further ordering'.[229] For the ancient Greeks, to be meant to be *physis* – i.e., things arising according to their own nature – and for the Medievals beings were divine creations; today, to be means to be standing-reserve.

Technology strives for maximum efficiency and convenience, which occurs when everything is so ordered that whatever we happen to need at the moment can be met immediately and effortlessly. All machines share the function of standing ready, waiting to fulfill our desires. The dishwasher crouches in the corner, waiting to spring into action the moment I want my dishes cleaned. And the water and electricity it requires must constantly stand at the edge of the faucet and socket, leaning forward in anticipation of service, ready to give their last full measure as soon as needed. Everything is organized around my gratification and my time-table; the more I have to do and the longer I have to wait to get what I want, the more I have to adapt my behaviour to the machines instead of the reverse, and thus the worse the technology.

Modern technology's great innovation lies in storing energy, the best possible resource since it is flexible enough to satisfy all kinds of purposes. We extract energy from nature and store it to be always on call for whatever task we happen to take up, making nature work around my schedule rather than the other way around. Instead of having to wait for the wind or the river to turn the mill, modern technology operates when I want it to, with a flip of a switch. Heidegger sees this as a profound change in our relationship to reality. An older 'machine' like a windmill is 'left entirely to the wind's blowing'.[230] Thanks to modern technology, I no longer need to regulate my desires and activities to conform to the seasons or the whims of nature; energy is ready when I want it. As figures like Descartes and Bacon promised at the dawn of the scientific revolution, nature has changed from our partner to our servant.

Revealing things as standing-reserve infects our relationship to everything. In order to produce the electricity that stands ready at my beck and call, I must see the raw materials as resources for fulfilling my desires. Ultimately, nature appears only as a resource to be transformed into more useful energy. Technology is really the means for converting less efficient forms of standing-reserve into more efficient forms since we come to see everything in these terms. As Heidegger puts it colourfully in a 1955 speech, 'nature becomes a gigantic gasoline station, an energy source for modern technology'.[231]

Let us now return to the distinction that opened the essay. The essence of technology goes far beyond just constructing and using machines; it is a more general attitude or way of revealing that has to precede their production and use. Before we can build agricultural gadgets to farm more efficiently, for instance, the earth must appear 'as a coal mining district, the soil as a mineral deposit. The field that the peasant formerly cultivated and set in order appears differently than it did' (320). This is why the essence of technology is a kind of revealing that enables the entire process of making and using machines in order to maximize our comfort. Standing-reserve is 'an inclusive rubric' (322); it takes over all of our thoughts about and interactions with beings: 'our whole human existence everywhere sees itself challenged . . . to devote itself to the planning and calculating of everything' (ID 34–5). Even 'current talk about human resources' (323) is no accident but an expression of how the attitude even extends to people. Many professors can attest to the way the vocation of teaching has become the academic 'business' ruled by the need to reduce waste and maximize output.

The essence of technology also forms the condition of modern science, rather than the reverse as common sense has it. Nature must stand ready to answer science's interrogations, preferably with simple useful answers. Scientific research enables us to use nature as energy only because it first reveals nature as conceptual standing-reserve: physics demands 'that nature . . . remain orderable as a system of information' (328). All mystery, anything that does not fit into systematic quantification, must be lopped off from true reality and relegated to the merely subjective.[232] Like Nietzsche, Levinas, and Foucault, Heidegger spots a hidden streak of aggression or violence within 'disinterested' inquiry.

Earlier, Heidegger conceded that the definition of technology as a human activity and a means to an end is 'correct' (313), but the subsequent ruminations have convinced him that 'the merely instrumental, merely anthropological definition of technology is therefore in principle untenable' (326). Although it captures the qualities common to technological apparatus, it misses the *essence* of technology. This is no small matter since all instrumental and anthropological technology presupposes the essence of technology as a way of revealing. Constructing machines is a human activity which we choose to do in order to achieve certain goals; we are in control of this. However, in order to be *capable* of this activity we must passively receive the manifestation of beings at all (the clearing), as well as their specific contemporary appearance as controllable (standing-reserve).

In principle, a clearing could not be 'constructed'. In order to create a site for beings to manifest themselves, we would have to already be aware that they exist and can become manifest to us, as well as whatever kinds of 'tools' or 'raw materials' were needed. But all of this presupposes the clearing. In order to make a clearing so that we could perceive the tools and raw materials, we would have to already reside within a clearing of some kind which itself could not have been made by us, on pain of infinite regress. Furthermore, beings would have to manifest themselves as desirable to discover, and the raw materials as useful for making a clearing. The essence of technology as a mode of unconcealment tends to expand to make everything seem under our control, 'but the unconcealment itself, within which ordering unfolds, is never a human handiwork'.[233] This essential and necessarily prior passivity of man, the necessary reception of the clearing as something neither of our making nor in our control, is one of the most prominent and pervasive themes of Heidegger's later work.

We can relate this notion to the four causes. In its Medieval adaptation, God as the ultimate efficient cause absorbs the other three: He determines the end of the universe (teleological), the Forms become Ideas in God's mind (formal), while pre-existing raw materials vanish when creation becomes *ex nihilo* (material). The divine efficient cause becomes the explanation for everything, the ultimate ground for the existence of all that is. And His causality is perfectly efficient; He simply says 'let there be light' and light appears.

Early modern thought maintains this emphasis on efficient causality with the goal of attaining power. Descartes' ambition to use technology to become lord and master of nature strives to close the gap between desire and fulfillment, which is achieved when we make light stream forth simply by flipping a switch. Being the controlling center of a web of willing and able machinery cultivates a sense of almost divine power where we are in charge of everything around us; with a hydro-electric dam spanning it, 'even the Rhine itself appears to be something at our command' (321). However, Heidegger's interpretation of the Greek doctrine of the four causes teaches us that efficient causality is just one factor in production which depends on the cooperation of the others and how they unconceal themselves. Materials must 'announce themselves' as resources and as put-togetherable-in such-and-such-a-way, structures must appear practical and promising, and goals desirable.

Thus not only are we thrown into the clearing or awareness in general, but we also find ourselves in the technological mode of unconcealment.

> If the Being of beings . . . did not already prevail, beings could not have appeared as objects, as what is objective in objects – and only by such objectivity do they become available to the ideas and propositions in the positing and disposing of nature by which we constantly take inventory of the energies we can wrest from nature. This disposition of nature according to its energy supply arises from the hidden essence of modern technology.[234]

By enabling us to control nature, technology fosters the sense that we are in complete control, in particular that we are in control of technology itself. We think of ourselves as the Kantian subject who is responsible for her clearing and its specific character, culminating in Nietzsche's dream that those strong enough may consciously control it. But for Heidegger, thrownness lies at the heart of any project (see, e.g., 234). We must be passively granted awareness since any attempt to bring it about would require awareness, as well as the specific way of thinking in terms of using resources for our purposes, i.e., the essence of technology.

The modern philosophy of subjectivity which portrays us as in control of the clearing begins when Descartes proposes to create a new way of thinking that will enable us to control nature better. The Aristotelian-Scholastic view of the world was useless so he set out to build a new kind of rationality or, in Heidegger's terms, a new clearing which could manipulate the world more efficiently and effectively. This ambition is announced in the very title of one of his books, *Rules for the Regulation of Reason*,[235] which could attain his goal to 'make ourselves, as it were, the lords and masters of nature'.[236] According to Heidegger's analysis, Descartes' procedure necessarily comes too late. In order even to want to create technology to control nature and to use a reformulated manner of thinking as the means to get it, these goals and materials must already announce themselves in a technological way, i.e., as means to the end of more efficient control. Thus, even to entertain the project of forging this new way of thinking, to find it plausible and desirable, indicates that one is already thinking in this new way.

So, according to Heidegger, all our ways of controlling the world around us are 'merely respond[ing] to the call of unconcealment' (324). We are always already within the clearing which cannot be our creation. Whatever is of our doing – our thoughts and our actions – are responses to the way beings present themselves. The modern world calls out to us to-be-controlled, materials announce themselves as to-be-put-together-and-used, which is what prompts us to engage in technological activity.

All action depends on this reception which enables and provokes our response, but the point has a special bite when applied to the modern clearing. Technology makes us think we are in control of everything but, ironically, we are not in control of being in control. This paradoxical state of affairs leads to some strange combinations of activity and passivity: 'man *finds himself* placed, on the basis of the being of beings, before the task of *undertaking mastery of the earth*.'[237] We are ordered to become masters, forced to force nature into our plan. The necessary condition of modern technology's willful autonomy is a heteronomous determination. He calls this 'challenging claim', i.e., the way that the essence of technology provokes this reaction, enframing (*Ge-stell*). 'Enframing . . . challenges [man] forth, to reveal the actual, in the mode of ordering, as standing-reserve . . . .. Technological activity . . . always merely responds to the challenge of enframing, but it never comprises enframing itself or brings it about' (325–6). We are challenged to challenge nature.

The project of autonomy, especially in the sense of taking control of one's own thoughts, runs throughout the history of philosophy, from Socrates chiding his fellow Athenians for not examining their beliefs, to Descartes doubting all of his beliefs in order to restock his mind in a well-ordered and controlled way, to Kant's insistence on both ethical and epistemological autonomy, to Nietzsche's encouragement to take control of one's own latent creative capacities. Heidegger, however, dismisses the idea as incoherent. We can only give ourselves a law on the basis of already being aware of the law and the law 'striking us' as good and right to follow. Although we may parade our beliefs before the tribunal of reason for approval or rejection, the judge's own authority cannot receive ultimate justification this way. The themes of mood (*Befindlichkeit*) and thrownness in Heidegger's early work now expand to encompass the particular ways of thinking we find appropriate. What we deem rational is a matter of what appeals most to our considered judgment. This does not rob our thinking of legitimacy, since there can be no higher court of appeals than what we ultimately find to be right.

III. RESPONDING TO THE CHALLENGE

Heidegger punctuates the essay with another break at page 328 and expresses dissatisfaction with the progress so far. He has determined the essence of technology to be enframing, a worrying condition, but we still do not know what to do about it (328). We have discovered that the essence of technology is a kind of revealing, one that challenges man to reveal nature in a challenging way. The question concerning technology now seems to be, how should we respond to this challenge? But in order to answer this, we must first gain a better understanding of what the challenge is. We can rule out the notion that enframing beings as standing-reserve falsifies them. Modern enframing *is* our unconcealment and hence is true; things now reveal themselves as standing-reserve and so they really are that kind of Being. Beings are as much standing-reserve today as they were divine creations in the Middle Ages and *physis* in ancient Greece (see 201).

It turns out that 'what is dangerous is not technology . . .. The essence of technology, as a destining of revealing, is the danger' (333). As usual, Heidegger is less concerned with 'ontic' problems like pollution than he is with the ontological issue of how Being comes to presence. This ontological issue presents two interdependent dangers. The first is the menace that haunts much of the later work – the forgetfulness of Being. As he states many times throughout his career, Being, the simple fact that beings are present to us, is very hard to attend to since we usually focus on the beings that are present. While this concern applies to all of Being's historical manifestations,[238] the modern epoch's understanding of Being is particularly prone to hide Being: 'when enframing holds sway, regulating and securing of the standing-reserve mark all revealing. They no longer even let their own fundamental characteristic appear, namely, this revealing as such'.[239]

Enframing forms a particularly strong concealment of unconcealment by fostering the sense that we create and control our mode of revealing. Since technology's goal is to maximize power through means that we make,

> man . . . exalts himself and postures as lord of the earth. In this way the illusion comes to prevail that everything man encounters exists only insofar as it is his construct . . . . Man stands so decisively in subservience to . . . the challenging-forth of enframing that he does not grasp enframing as a claim, that he fails to see himself as the one spoken to.[240]

Viewing ourselves as in control of our thinking and the source of our clearing blocks the realization that these have been conferred upon us, that Being is 'given' to us (this is the more literal translation of 'es gibt Sein'). Although Heidegger repeatedly rejects the attempt to compare epochal understandings, both Greek *physis* and Medieval divine creation are more amenable to this realization than enframing. At least these earlier understandings of Being see things and meaning arising from a source other than ourselves, making wonder and gratitude appropriate, if somewhat misplaced and misinterpreted, responses. If, on the other hand, it is all our doing, there is no room for gratitude or feeling responsible for taking care of our boon.

Let us contrast a traditional farmer with a modern scientist raising plants. The farmer knows down to his bones that he is completely dependent on nature's cooperation, and this shapes how he works. 'In sowing grain [the peasant] places seed in the keeping of the forces of growth and watches over its increase'.[241] It needs some rain but not too much, some sunshine but not too much, richness in the soil, etc. If any of these factors is out of proportion to the crop's needs, there is little he can do. On the other hand, if the modern technological agriculturist's plants need water, she simply turns on the sprinkler and water immediately bursts forth. If they need light, she flips a switch and light beams down on them. Hydroponic growing even does away with the ground as an inefficient medium. The overall effect is to instill the feeling that she is in total control of the process and that she unilaterally creates the end product, the way the efficient cause swallowed up the other causes. Heidegger points out that at the heart of all of this control, the scientist is as dependent as the farmer on the brute fact that plants grow under these conditions. She does not create the process of organic growth, but just makes the circumstances optimally conducive for the plant to grow. If it were to change its normal behaviour for some unknown reason, she would be powerless to force it to grow; natural disasters often impart this sense of the usually ignored limitations of technology. No matter how effective, the efficient cause always needs the cooperation of the others.

Thus, both the scientist and the farmer are really in a partnership with the plant, but only the farmer knows this. Heidegger argues that although we are the ones who dig the coal out of the ground, burn it, and transform its energy into the more useful form of electricity, this is not creation but merely transformation. We depend on coal being combustible in specific, stable, usable ways which we did not create. Technology fosters the illusion that we are in complete control, but in principle we can only cooperate with what the available resources and the laws of nature yield.[242] 'Only a minute fraction of what lies before us in this way has been laid down by man, and even then only with the aid of what was lying there before. The stones from which the house is built come from the natural rock' (WCT 200). In the language of 'The Origin of the Work of Art', the farmer maintains the strife between world and earth, whereas the scientist futilely tries to absorb earth into world; in the terms of *Being and Time*, we can only project what we have been thrown into.

The second feature of the ontological danger relates to Heidegger's idea that every revealing is at the same time a concealing;[243] seeing something as one kind of being excludes seeing it as any other kind. On a larger scale, each epoch's understanding of Being prevents us from experiencing the others. Heidegger plays on the etymological connection of the word 'epoch' with '*epochē*' to suggest the bracketing or withdrawal that characterizes all clearings (see N 4:239). Just as all epochs forget Being but the modern era is particularly prone to do so, the same is true of the way that all epochs block other modes of appearing. 'Where this ordering holds sway, it drives out every other possibility of revealing'.[244] Enframing is a jealous clearing, demanding that we have no other clearings alongside it. This is clearly visible in scientism, the view that science tells us all there is to know about the world. No understanding of Being is false, but neither can any be considered the single absolute truth; any claim to be the one true revelation should be rejected.

These two aspects of the danger posed by enframing – (1) its concealment of Being as the source of all understandings, and (2) its insistence on being the one true understanding – are interconnected. 'The challenging-enframing not only conceals [2] a former way of revealing (bringing-forth [i.e., Greek *poiēsis*]) but also [1] conceals revealing itself and with it that wherein unconcealment, i.e., truth, propriates' (333). We can see how this happens in Kant for instance: it is because (1) we are the source of the formal features of experience that (2) these and only these features are necessary and universal to our experience. On the other hand, if our clearing descends upon us from Being, then a new one could occur at any time (thus reintroducing the Humean contingency that Kant seeks to eliminate). 'If Enframing is a destining of the coming to presence of Being itself, then we may venture to suppose that Enframing, as one among Being's modes of coming to presence, changes' (QT 37).

Now that we understand the danger better, we should be able to figure out how to fix the problem, but Heidegger introduces a twist here. Just as Descartes' drive to change his own thinking to the technological comes too late, so any attempt to overcome technology necessarily comes too early. Trying to bend technology to our will in order to render it harmless is itself an expression of the technological attitude. 'The instrumental conception of technology conditions every attempt to bring man into the right relation to technology . . .. We will, as we say, "get" technology "intelligently in hand". We will master it'.[245] This very way of framing the problem and setting about fixing it is guided by the technological attitude, and so can only perpetuate it instead of overcoming it. Because enframing as the essence of technology consists in viewing issues as problems to be solved by taking action, 'human activity can never directly counter this danger' (339). One way that the essence of technology differs from technology is that it cannot be dealt with the way that technological issues are without perpetuating the danger, thus somewhat justifying Heidegger's disdain for ontic problems. As long as we ignore the ontological issue, no decisive change can happen.

Heidegger follows a line of Hölderlin's poetry which implies that 'precisely the essence of technology must harbor in itself the growth of the saving power'.[246] Instead of trying to fix technology, which would treat it as under our control and thereby perpetuate the technological way of seeing the world, we should turn to the essence of technology. Whereas technology's astonishing power allows us to feel in control, the *essence* of technology as a way of revealing is neither our creation nor under our control. This allows us to 'experience enframing as a destining of revealing' (330). The German word translated here as 'destining' (*'Geschick'*) has strong connections to 'what is fitting, suitable, appropriate' (*'schicklich'*), as well as to both 'sending' (*'Schicken'*) and history (*'Geschichte'*).[247] The particular clearing sent to us at this point in history is what makes us who we are; it is our destiny.

It is tempting to read all of this in terms of traditional notions of destiny, which yields a mystical Heidegger telling (ontotheological) stories of a super-Being sending our destiny to us. But we have to remember that, according to the ontological difference, Being is not a being; it is not God or a god or any kind of separate agent performing actions (see 331). Like Nietzsche, Heidegger fights the substance-ontology built into the grammar of our language which implies that every action arises from a distinct agent. As discussed in 'Letter on Humanism', Be-ing as sender is not separable from the sending or from what is sent. 'Nothing that effects, as Being, precedes the mode in which it – Being itself – takes place so as to adapt itself; and no effect, as Being, follows after. Sheerly, out of its own essence of concealedness, Being brings itself to pass into its epoch.'[248] Being is not in any way a being; it does not exist apart from man nor is it any kind of agent. Rather, Be-ing *is* presencing in the clearing that we are. We receive the clearing as something that is not our creation but which determines us through and through (337). Heidegger wants to remove the clearing from our imagined control, undermining the technological illusion that we are in complete control of the world and ourselves.

He is also playing on the sense of mystery contained in the traditional notion of destiny. The epochs of Being resist our attempts to comprehend why they are the way they are, or to place them in a logical order.[249] As the source of our rationality, our clearing cannot itself be explained, nor can we apply a particular epoch's understanding to that which grants all understanding. Heidegger rejects Hegel's attempt to make the historical changes in thinking into a rational evolution, claiming instead that, 'the surmounting of a destining of Being . . . each time comes to pass out of the arrival of another destining, a destining that does not allow itself either to be logically and historiographically predicted or to be metaphysically construed as a sequence belonging to a process of history'.[250] Being thrown into a particular way of reasoning, we find certain ways of arguing plausible and others ridiculous, some types of evidence persuasive and some irrelevant.[251] But these ways of thinking cannot themselves be justified without employing either these ways of thinking or retreating to another beginning point which then would stand in need of justification itself. The appropriate way to think of Being preserves its mysteriousness, the way philosophy respects untruth in 'On the Essence of Truth' and artworks bring earth into the open as the self-closing.[252]

Heidegger is not completely consistent in his analysis of the history of thinking. On the one hand, he wants to avoid a Hegelian pattern of epochs, often calling the switch between them a leap or a chasm to indicate the impossibility of a bridge making them continuous. In Kuhn's terminology, different eras are incommensurable and hence cannot be compared or joined into an overall trend. On the other hand, sometimes he does suggest a tenuous connection among them. 'The epochs can never be derived from one another much less be placed on the track of an ongoing process. Nevertheless, there is a legacy [*Überlieferung*] from epoch to epoch'.[253] It is this 'legacy' that allows him to write narratives of the intelligible or even inevitable development (usually decline) of the history of philosophy, where Plato's initial distinction between Being and appearance contains all future variations in embryo, up to Nietzsche's ultimate reversal of the two.

Finally, Heidegger invokes destiny's connotation that our lives are watched over by benevolent beings. He wants us to see the sendings as gifts for which we should be grateful, even though there is not anyone to be grateful to. The essay ends with the hope to 'awaken and found anew our vision of, and trust in, that which grants' (340). Even though the modern clearing of enframing is 'the danger', it is still a revelation of Being and so should be treasured. We cannot scoff at the particular epoch we have been thrown into but should gratefully safeguard the clearing that we have.

> Every destining of revealing propriates from a granting and as such a granting . . .. The granting that sends one way or another into revealing is as such the saving power. For the saving power lets man see and enter into the highest dignity of his essence.[254]

Having a clearing at all is such an awesome event that we should never stop wondering at it or being grateful for it, although this above all things is usually taken for granted. Our 'ethical task' is to dwell in and nurture our awareness the way the farmer cultivates a seed.[255]

This attitude is what can overcome nihilism. Heidegger argues that the idea that all values come from human valuing, the key to Nietzsche's attempt to overcome nihilism, actually represents the ultimate form of nihilism. As finite mortals, we are simply unable to sustain value in the world in such a way that will make a good, meaningful life on our own; values that result from our choices cannot obligate us or fill us with awe. We need tradition, community, and the natural patterns the ancients called *'cosmos logos'*. For Heidegger, there is something profoundly comforting in the fact that the epochs come to us, that ultimately we are not in control, which is why overcoming the oblivion of Being is at the same time the overcoming of nihilism. Although the concepts of benevolence or malevolence cannot really apply to Being as the source of the 'sendings', the epochal understandings furnish us with whatever meaningfulness we find in this life, making them the greatest gifts possible. The fact that, in principle, we cannot alter our clearing, combined with this inculcation of trusting gratitude for however things appear to us, make up what is called later Heidegger's 'quietism'.

STUDY QUESTIONS

1   Why can't we overcome technology by our own efforts?
2   Explain standing-reserve. Describe something that is not usually considered technology as standing-reserve.
3   What is the difference between technology and the essence of technology? What are they? Why is this distinction so important?

g. Building Dwelling Thinking

Initially this essay may read like a perplexing poetic ramble circling around two obscure groups of terms – the fourfold and dwelling/building/locale – which bear little discernible relation to each other. Fortunately, much of the work becomes intelligible once one sees how it develops Heidegger's more straightforward phenomenological descriptions of space in *Being and Time*[256] and 'Modern Science, Metaphysics, and Mathematics', which may serve as helpful background readings. The fourfold is a new idea in Heidegger's later thought that plays a prominent role in several essays of the fifties, and I must admit that I feel less confidence in my grasp of it than just about any other notion in *Basic Writings*.

The opening paragraph of the essay asks what dwelling is and how building belongs to it, and each of the two sections making up the body of the essay responds to one of these questions. However, if building does belong to dwelling, as the second question suggests, then we will not be able to answer the first question with an isolated definition just of dwelling. We will only understand dwelling if we also come to understand building, and both efforts may require a rethinking of thinking. Thus, from the essay's very beginning, even its first sentence, we find the three titular terms interconnected. This holism, i.e., the idea that parts can only be grasped by locating them in the whole to which they belong, runs throughout the essay.

I. WHAT IS IT TO DWELL?

Following his usual procedure of starting with the common or average everyday understanding of a topic, Heidegger first lays out the standard view of the relationship between building and dwelling: we construct certain kinds of buildings such as houses so that we may live within them. Building functions as the means to secure the end of dwelling, two independent actions brought into an instrumental connection for a specific goal. While this is in some sense correct, it also covers over essential features, 'for building is not merely a means and a way toward dwelling – to build is in itself to dwell'.[257] The holistic interconnection between the two undermines this depiction of a means-ends relationship between entirely separate activities.

This objection receives its justification from language which 'tells us about the essence of a thing'.[258] Especially in his later work, Heidegger takes etymology very seriously for at least two reasons. First, language is often misconceived as merely a means to express an internal idea[259] – the vehicle for ideas traveling from mind to mind. Like many twentieth-century philosophers, Heidegger believes that we can only think linguistically, that rather than a neutral transparent medium, language's own characteristics necessarily inform our thinking.[260] Second, Heidegger sometimes describes the initial coinage of words as penetrating mini-descriptions of fresh experiences of phenomena before they get dulled by continuous handling or hijacked by standard views. Although etymology cannot serve as proof, excavating the insights captured in these 'essential words'[261] frequently yields important suggestions. In this case, the fact that the Old High German word for building also means to dwell supplies the clue (349).

A closer examination of building uncovers its two varieties: the cherishing, protective way that farmers cultivate crops, and the construction of edifices like houses. Despite their differences, both kinds of building are forms of dwelling.[262] We miss this because the way we carry out our everyday lives inconspicuously 'recedes' (349), making it hard to grasp how we actually experience the world. The elusiveness of the mundane inspires and guides phenomenology in general, and it runs throughout

Heidegger's career. As the Introduction to *Being and Time* states, that which pervades every moment of our lives is, for that very reason, hardest to think about.[263] Then, when we do try to think about and articulate how we live in the world, we tend to misconstrue it profoundly, giving rise to the chronic errors that clog the history of philosophy.

Dwelling recedes by dispersing into the various activities and projects we pursue, including building, which hide their fundamental unity. Remarking on the etymological proximity between the words for dwelling and being, Heidegger argues that dwelling is the way that we *are*, our 'Being' or 'basic character'.[264] Dwelling is so essential to who we are that it accounts for all of our behaviour. Like all of our basic actions, we can only understand building in light of dwelling, justifying his earlier rejection of their common sense means-ends relationship: 'we do not dwell because we have built, but we build and have built because we dwell, that is, because we are *dwellers*' (350). Dwelling is how we *are*, which informs everything we do. Therefore, we must grasp any particular behaviour in light of dwelling, the subject of the essay's first question.

Another brief etymological discussion links dwelling to peace, to the free, to sparing, concluding that dwelling should be understood as sparing (351). Just as letting be does not mean apathetic indifference in 'On the Essence of Truth',[265] so here sparing does not leave things alone. Genuine sparing helps something achieve its own essence, rather like the way cultivating facilitates plants growing towards their *telos*. This sparing suffuses all that we do, so we might get a better sense of it by taking another look at our behaviour in general, which gets unified by dwelling. Now, however, Heidegger emphasizes that dwelling means 'the stay of mortals on the earth' (351). And a shift in the essay occurs here by means of the holistic notion that we only comprehend individual items in relation to their opposing term: so we understand what mortals are by way of divinities, and earth once it has been paired with sky. In fact, all four belong together so that none can exist or make sense unless encompassed in their '*primal oneness*'.[266] We have now moved from dwelling-building to one of Heidegger's most obscure ideas: the fourfold.

Heidegger briefly discusses the four components one by one, but insists at the end of each description that talking about any one of them involves the other three.[267] Although we can only focus on one at a time, their deep unity must always be kept in mind.[268] Earth focuses on natural growth and abundance (with a whiff of *physis*), while sky seems to indicate nature's inherent patterns, what the Greeks called the *'cosmos logos'*, i.e., the intelligible structure of the universe evinced in phenomena like the regularity of the seasons. Mortals are 'capable of death *as* death' (352) in that, unlike animals, we know that we will die.[269] Heidegger often associates the gods with the sense of the world as meaningful, while their loss amounts to something akin to nihilism.[270]

The fourfold represents something like the 'logical space' organizing our lives and projects. In the connected essay, 'Poetically Man Dwells', the four elements create a 'spanning' or 'between . . . measured out for the dwelling of man'.[271] We live out our lives within the place stretched out between these general features of our existence: after birth and before death, on the earth and under the sky, too late for the old gods and too early for a new holiness (PLT 4), between the conditions that make us what we are and what we make out of these conditions – i.e., between thrownness and projection. We are riddled with needs (ultimately leading to death), placed on a fecund earth whose cycles we can grasp and cooperate with. We are the animals who know that we are fated to die, as well as the beings who await the divine blessing of a meaningful life.

Dwelling now appears as safeguarding the fourfold. We dwell by letting these dimensions come into their essence each in its own way. While they vary, in each case we let the dimension unfold itself rather than forcing our desires or expectations onto it. Saving the earth means working it without exhausting it, unlike technological mastery which treats land merely as a resource to be maximally exploited (320). Receiving the sky refrains from disrupting the natural patterns of night and day by lighting up the night for our convenience or squeezing every second of productivity out of a day. We await divinities instead of creating gods or determining our own ultimate values, as Nietzsche recommends. Initiating our death secures 'a good death' (352) at home among family and friends, instead of desperately clinging to survival in a sterile hospital. Every case of preserving consists in letting be, allowing each dimension to present itself in its own way rather than steamrolling over its intrinsic tendencies to get what we want.

This sparing cannot accept the fourfold abstractly, but must take place with particular beings, namely, things.[272] We can only let the fourfold flower in our dealings with things, and even then only when we allow them to be truly things (353). Safeguarding things means letting them fully be themselves and, when this is done, they in turn allow the fourfold. Among the ways in which we let things be are the two types of building, leading to an enriched version of the conclusion reached earlier: *'dwelling*, inasmuch as it keeps the fourfold in things, is, as this keeping, a *building'* (353). This connection now brings us to the essay's second question.

II. HOW DOES BUILDING BELONG TO DWELLING?

Since dwelling only happens with things and, more specifically, when they are fully allowed to be things, we now turn to them. Unfortunately, philosophers have long represented things very differently from the way we experience them. In particular substance ontology defines things as an objective base supporting qualities. This conception divides features into those that really belong to the thing and those that are 'afterward read into it',[273] somewhat like Locke's distinction between primary and secondary qualities. Only certain features enjoy the status of true reality, while the rest of our experience of things gets demoted to merely subjective projections. Heidegger's phenomenological approach, on the other hand, accepts all that shows itself as real. Since the theoretical attitude shears off so much the richness of our experience, Heidegger says that our thinking traditionally *'understates'* the essence of things.[274] Like *Being and Time*, much of this essay consists in contrasting the theoretical conception of things with how they actually appear in our normal but inconspicuous encounters with them.

What it means to be a thing is to gather the fourfold in a particular way,[275] and Heidegger briefly (and rather obscurely) shows how his chosen example of a bridge treats each element with respect.[276] This gathering organizes the surrounding area into a new arrangement. According to a kind of Gestalt theory of perception, installing the bridge fundamentally changes the landscape into which it has been placed, creating a new whole which is more than just the sum of the bridge and the environment. Instead of simply joining the pre-existing banks over a river, 'the banks emerge as banks only as the bridge crosses the stream . . .. The bridge *gathers* the earth as landscape around the stream' (354). Once it has been erected, the bridge retroactively brings about its setting.[277]

This organization has effects that refute our usual means-ends outlook.[278] We normally think of something like a bridge as a tool we use in pursuing our projects, in this case crossing the river to gather wood or crops and bringing them to town to sell. But Heidegger attributes much of what we think of as our agency to the thing, rendering our actions responses to the environment's 'solicitations'. Instead of our autonomously deciding upon a goal and then constructing or employing the means necessary to achieve it, Heidegger says that 'the bridge initiates the lingering and hastening ways of men to and fro' (354). This transference of agency from an ego regally determining her own actions to 'external' forces – language, things, Being – is an important part of Heidegger's anti-humanism, i.e., his attack on traditional conceptions of human nature.

He introduces two technical terms here to illuminate how buildings perform this function: 'things which, as locales, allow a site we now in anticipation call buildings' (356). The bridge is a locale in that it sets up a site, which is an area arranged so as to make sense to people and to make sense of their lives. The bridge organizes the world of those who live there by lighting up some jobs and destinations while drawing attention away from others: 'by this site are determined the places and paths by which a space is provided for' (356). The bridge unifies the area, laying out the tasks of carrying crops to the city or seed to the fields, coloring in what lies on the near side as home and the far side as the outside. 'Things such as locales shelter or house men's lives' by the 'founding and joining of spaces', setting out and organizing the projects, values, and meanings within which we live.[279] The area is now divided into places or qualitative zones: friendly and hostile, work and rest, familiar and strange.

Now, just as things can be treated either as theoretical objects or as living breathing parts of our everyday lives, so the value-laden space we live in can be reduced to mathematically expressible extension for theoretical analysis. Descartes initiated this latter perspective by defining physical objects as inert matter occupying exact positions within a featureless, homogeneous, neutral grid. Like substance ontology, this view sorts out real objective features from subjective projections so that 'nearness and remoteness between men and things can become mere distance'.[280]

We should not be bullied by the usefulness or universal applicability of theoretical space into ceding it full reality, while relegating all the usual meaningful features that we actually live and work and move around in to the merely subjective.[281]

We must un-cover this lived-space we dwell in that remains beneath the theoretical notion of space by examining 'the spaces through which we go daily', which 'are provided for by locales . . . grounded in things of the type of buildings' (358). Whereas Cartesian space is a homogeneous container which neither affects nor is affected by what it contains, our lived space unfolds from and around buildings. Moreover, just as *Being and Time* posits a lived-time in which the three tenses intermingle instead of the theoretical conception of a sequence of discrete now-points,[282] so lived-space is not defined by the rules of geometry or physics. Rather than being a self-enclosed substantial ego occupying one point in space, we ek-sist which means that we stand outside ourselves with other beings. Rather than just 'this encapsulated body' at this objective position, 'I already pervade the space of the room' (359). Just as *Being and Time* argues that I live predominantly in the future, grasping my present situation in anticipation of my goals, so I am spatially 'nearer' to the object of my concern than I am to my present position to which I give little thought. Entities located next to me, my glasses, say, or my shoes, are remote in lived-space if I pay little attention to them.[283]

Heidegger rejects the Cartesian picture of subjects facing bare material objects whose only meaning is what we endow them with in an endless featureless space. Rather, we dwell in a community, within the natural rhythms of seasons and growth/decay, in a world charged with meaning. In his earlier work he called this context of significance the world; here he calls it the fourfold of earth, sky, mortals, and divinities.[284] In this essay, as in much of his work, Heidegger attempts to call our attention to what we take for granted in all of our behaviour and which escapes the theoretical gaze. The emphasis here is on the role played by the space laid out by buildings. Our lives take place within a 'rapport with things', which can evaporate 'in states of depression' or during theoretical analysis but which defines our normal behaviour.[285] Taking these perceptions as authoritative, as science (and Sartre and Nietzsche) argue for, puts us on the road to the subject-object picture with all its many implications. However, as Heidegger says many times, such breakdowns allow us to see what was there all along. These anxious/depressed and theoretical views of bare objects should not be taken for the true reality, but seen as the impoverished substitute that it is. Such greyness of objects should point us to the technicolour of things that is our usual habitat. These are the things that provide locales within which we know our way around, that give us directives and guide our actions, that are-to-be-valued or simply do not catch our attention rather maintaining a static presence.

In the related essay 'The Thing', Heidegger says that 'thinking in this way, we are called by the thing as the thing. In the strict sense of the German word *bedingt*, we are the be-thinged, the conditioned ones. We have left behind us the presumption of all unconditionedness.'[286] This last sentence is particularly important as a summary manifesto of Heidegger's repeated attempts to rethink traditional notions of freedom and rationality within the context of the radical finitude, dependence, and inescapable conditionedness that form the human condition. Instead of compromising us somehow, this conditionedness is a necessary condition for us to think and act. In order for us to build, we must find this action appropriate, we must need or want what the building will accomplish, and an appropriate location must solicit us to build there. Building *receives the directive* for its erecting of locales'.[287] Building is a response to the conditions we always operate under and within. Being receptive to these directives, callings, and inherent significance is part of what it means to dwell (360–1). The fact that these directives and meanings prompt us to build undermines the means-ends way of understanding the relationship between building and dwelling.[288] We dwell – i.e., we find within ourselves needs, desires, preferences, etc. – which then pushes us towards performing various actions, among which is the organization of spaces and the building of buildings in order to meet these needs. If we had not had these needs or, like many animals, found ourselves disposed to fulfill them in different ways, we would never have built at all.

I find the essay's second example of a building, an old farmhouse in the Black Forest, far more convincing and illuminating of how things gather the fourfold. Its location – sheltered from the wind by the mountain and facing the meadows – reveals the earth's cooperation which the peasants use without trying to control it. The house's structure protects it from the sky's weather without fully removing it; their winter nights remain long, whereas artificial heat and light remake ours into more convenient periods. The 'altar corner' gives a place to the gods, whose presence is shown by the way the house accommodates mortals. Having both crib and coffin in the same house 'designed for the different generations under one roof the character of their journey through time' (362). The generations living together highlights the various stages of life and, in particular, their continuity. Hiding the dead, aged, and infirm fosters the illusion of an indefinite extension of the present, while the peasant children see their destiny in the elders and the dead. Due to the spatial arrangement of their home, life appears as an organized whole, rather than an ongoing now-point. In describing how buildings shape spaces meaningfully, Heidegger made the point that boundaries are not limitations but are what gives a thing its identity (356); the farmhouse does this for a life.

Although he often idealizes the past, either ancient Greece or Germany's feudal peasants, Heidegger consistently rejects the notion of returning to earlier times (see 362). The farmhouse serves as an illuminating example of dwelling, not the right way to live which we need to resurrect. We need to learn to dwell in our lives with all of their distinctive features instead of simply occupying them. This, and not housing shortages, represents the true housing problem.[289] Although all of our actions are grounded on the context of intelligibility and significance we find ourselves in, we think of these features as dependent on us – on our autonomous rational thought and freely willed decisions. Thanks to our rapport with things, thanks to the very conditionedness that philosophy's quest for autonomy has tried to slough off, we live in a world filled with meaning. We have to realize this and cherish it, which we can do through thinking about it. As he says in an essay from 1955, 'thinking and poetizing must return to where, in a certain way, they have always already been but have never yet built. Only through building, however, can we prepare a dwelling in that locality.'[290]

STUDY QUESTIONS

1 Why is building already a dwelling?
2 Pick an example of a successful building you are familiar with and describe how it gathers the fourfold.
3 Explain the differences between Cartesian space and Heidegerrian space.

h. The Way to Language

The title of this essay suggests that we need a way to get to language as if it were a distant destination that we must travel to (397). But of course, just being able to read the essay shows that in some sense we already possess language, making a journey to it appear unnecessary. Although speech has long been considered our defining trait as the *zoon logicon*, Heidegger doubts that we have a proper relationship to language which would enable us to experience it as it really is (398). The fact that we are linguistic to our core actually hinders our attempt to grasp language since, as he frequently says, what is nearest to us is for that very reason farthest away. We rarely notice and, when we do, we have difficulty articulating pervasive phenomena such as our own way of Being (54), Being itself (234), and now language. So while we obviously do not need a way to language in the sense of first attaining speech, we do need to reach it as it really is. He puts his goal in an essay called 'Language' this way: 'we would like only, for once, to get to just where we are already'.[291] Although we are immersed in language, we lack a proper understanding of it which, if achieved, will transform our relation to language and, ultimately, our lives as a whole.

Heidegger describes the essay's project as the attempt '*to bring language as language to language*' (398). Such Dr. Seussian repetition is just the kind of wording that makes many readers suspicious that he is engaging in intentional obfuscation for the appearance of profundity. But when you slow down and pay attention the phrase actually makes perfect sense. The first part, 'to bring language', simply specifies the subject matter: we are talking about language here. *Talking* about it, of course, means bringing it 'to language'. Even if there is a level of pre-linguistic awareness to our actions, as some contend (and as some attribute to Heidegger), certainly all higher order thinking occurs in language. Understanding these kinds of topics means giving a *logos* or linguistic account of them.

It is the middle phrase—'bringing language *as language* to language'—that perplexes. How else can we study something than by talking about it *as* itself? Well, Heidegger repeatedly argues that most philosophical and mundane interpretations approach their object with the wrong horizon, i.e., they use the wrong concepts to view and explain the topic. Perhaps the main point of *Being and Time* (as we have it) is that we mis-take ourselves as tools or objects, whereas our way of Being is so distinctive that it demands its own set of concepts.[292] The first section of 'The Origin of the Work of Art' shows at some length how artworks defy the categories of things and tools, thus demonstrating the need for their own terms.[293] Examples can be multiplied. The phenomenological motto, 'to the things themselves', means, among other things, that we must employ the appropriate horizon in order to capture a phenomenon faithfully. Thus, bringing language to language *as language*, i.e., talking about language *within the right horizon*, is absolutely essential and surprisingly rare. Similar to his treatment of art in 'The Origin of the Work of Art', the first section of this essay shows how Western philosophy has consistently conceived of language not as language but as something else, which dooms all attempts to understand it.

I. SECTION I

At their 'acme', the ancient Greeks saw language as a way of showing and letting appear (thereby producing *alētheia*) but then, perhaps in the Classical era, they started understanding language in terms of designation. This alteration results from their conception of truth changing from unconcealment to correspondence, one of the most significant events in Western history for Heidegger.[294] Words become things that refer to other things. Language hooks the set of words up with the set of referents, and truth consists in the correct correlation between sentences and states of affairs. Heidegger believes that this view has dominated Western thought, culminating in Wilhelm von Humboldt's work,[295] making it the proper place to demonstrate the conception's problems.

Humboldt does not think about language as language because he starts from a detailed quasi-Kantian or Hegelian theory of human conception which shapes all of his ideas. In line with this modern philosophy of subjectivity, Humboldt traces everything back to the subject's activity. Instead of being studied for its own sake, language only represents one instance of subjectivity's behavior (405). Heidegger's opening prescription to bring language *as language* to language appears more substantial in light of the fact that Humboldt fails to do this, instead bringing language *as* the subject's activity *to* the language of modern metaphysics.

II. SECTION II

The second section of 'The Way to Language' begins by repeating the essay's guiding instruction to avoid alien horizons or general notions which language instantiates in order 'to let language be experienced as language'.[296] Now that we have cleared away these misguided attempts to understand language in terms of something else, we can begin thinking about it in its own terms. As in *Being and Time*'s analysis of Dasein (BT 69/43), Heidegger examines the phenomenon in its 'average everydayness', i.e., how it occurs in its usual mundane contexts, with the goal of finding what unifies all of these features. Language occurs primarily and for the most part in our speech (406). Of course, we must now avoid another traditional misconception of speech, namely 'the phonetic, acoustic, physiological explanation' which presents speech as 'the creation of sounds' (408). Speaking does make sounds of course, but that is not how we experience it primarily and for the most part.[297] This characterization is the kind of third person objective account that phenomenologists bracket in favor of describing how we actually experience the phenomenon.

Speech occurs in our lives as a way to relate to beings. Talking about things makes them present to ourselves and to others. When I tell you that my dog has brown and black fur, I present him to you; making small talk forms a connection between speakers without transferring any real informational content ('pretty hot today, huh?'[298]). Speaking of something points it out or highlights it, loosening or 'freeing' it from its previously seamless integration into the unnoticed background. The noise the refrigerator is making or the feel of your shoes suddenly step out from the undifferentiated surroundings to make a demand on your attention when commented on. Accordingly, Heidegger defines language as a kind of showing or 'pointing, reaching out to every region of presencing, letting what is present in each case appear in such regions'.[299]

A surprising phrase turns up in the course of this discussion: 'it is language that speaks.'[300] The common sense and traditional view is that language is a tool by which we express what goes on inside of us. Besides all of the problems associated with the notion of a private internal event getting labeled and then exported to other minds,[301] Heidegger takes great exception to the notion that language is entirely up to us.[302] Much of his later work expounds the notion sometimes called 'anti-humanism' which attacks the view of ourselves as autonomous self-transparent subjects in total control of what we do, say, think, etc.[303]

Although words often feel like pure crystalline meaning that springs forth spontaneously from our minds, expression has to take place within a fairly determinate vocabulary in line with a fairly firm grammar for communication to work. Only certain arrangements of words successfully express something and only a small minority of grammatically correct statements can be made in any context without provoking funny looks and confusion. Only the relatively tiny set of statements in accord with the speaker's epochal understanding of Being are acceptable. A scientific principle which is 'self-evident' to us, e.g., would not even rise to the level of falsity for preceding eras, but rather remain 'senseless' in the absence of an appropriate way of thinking (see 280). Thus, at the heart of what seems most our own, we find ourselves constrained by an alien vocabulary and grammar, by structures of intelligibility we have inherited rather than created. Our private, personal speech is really the activation of norms and rules that we did not make. 'We not only *speak* language, we speak *from out of* it. We are capable of doing so only because in each case we have already listened to language.'[304] Successful speech-acts obey a massive shared set of conventions.

Poets, portrayed by Romantic theories of genius as heroically dominating language to forge utterly original and personal expressions, actually submit the most to language. Poets do not put words in a headlock to force them to do their bidding, but rather pay careful attention to linguistic nuances. Sensitive listening, the ability to discern subtle shades of meaning, and the willingness to let words guide them are the qualities that distinguish good poets. 'The more poetic a poet is . . . the greater is the purity with which he submits what he says to an ever more painstaking listening.'[305] But this is just an extreme form of what we all do whenever we speak, which is why speaking is always a form of listening.

In addition to compliance with these standards, there is a deeper way that speaking is a listening. As previously discussed, describing a scene shows it to my interlocutors, but I can only tell them what has shown itself to me. Just as in Heidegger's analysis of correspondence truth assertions can only correspond to something that has manifested itself,[306] so too we can only talk about something if it has shown itself to us. Not only must it have appeared, but the particular details pointed out must have already called attention to themselves as relevant. My dog's fur announces itself as brown and black, as well as deserving discussion; if it had not, I would not have noticed it or thought it worth mentioning. In conversations, we end up 'showing one another the sorts of things that are suggested by what is addressed in our discussion, showing one another what the addressed allows to radiate of itself' (409). I warn someone of a slippery patch in the hall for example because it presents itself to me as dangerous and important, the kind of thing one ought to alert others to. My speech is and can only be a reaction to how the world presents itself to me; 'every spoken word is already a response.'[307]

If our assertions are to correspond to the world, as the traditional theory of truth has it, then the world has to present itself to me in representable ways. The world must possess a grammar, that we can say it; it *'lets itself be told'* (411). This is Heidegger's take on the twofold meaning of *'logos'* as both language and rational structure—speaking about the world requires that it present itself in an intelligible and sayable form. Heidegger makes this point with the term 'rift-design' ('*Aufriss*'), which refers both to drawings and the act of ripping, as in farmers cutting lines in a field to render it open to life-sustaining growth. I think that what Heidegger is getting at here is captured by our word 'articulate', which means both the property of being made up of distinct parts and the act of expressing an idea in language. A skeleton is articulate because neatly divisible into discrete units, while a person is articulate by being able to describe the articulations of the world correctly and thoroughly. The intelligibility of the world and the words we use to say it are inextricably intertwined.[308]

By this point, an apparent contradiction has arisen. On the one hand, Heidegger argues that language depends on a prior appearance of reality, giving language a mimetic or mirroring function which 'is preceded by a thing's letting itself be shown'.[309] On this reading, things present themselves to us with certain qualities shining out as relevant, as to-be-noticed-and-communicated, leaving our speech to 'reiterate the saying we have heard' (411).

On the other hand, Heidegger also talks about language as what initially opens up and articulates the world, so that we can only perceive what has been singled out and named. Language points, 'letting what is present in each case appear'.[310] This view, sometimes called linguistic idealism, claims that our ability to discern and think about various features of reality is a product of and correlates with our vocabulary. Our basic acquisition of words took place early on, making our linguistic clearing one of those things we are 'always already' within, but taking a wine appreciation course presents an object lesson: you learn to pick out previously imperceptible shades of taste as you master a set of terms (high and low notes, woody, complexity, etc.). These words play a necessary role in taste detection so that you come to discriminate finer shades as you acquire their names, while perception and thinking become cruder as your vocabulary thins out, eventually collapsing into the merely formal category of 'something'. On this view, reality does not simply fall into a predetermined set of objects on its own, like the animals waiting for Adam to name them, but comes into greater resolution as our language becomes more precise and sophisticated.

So which view is right? Does reality precede language or does language initially unconceal reality? Heidegger actually dismisses the question of which grounds which because in this 'search for grounds we pass on by the essence of language' (412). I take this to mean that he regards the question of whether reality grounds language or language grounds reality as a bad question. Language's relationship to Being is not amenable to causal or chronological analysis; language reveals Being *and* Being tells language what to say. Although we have the urge to stop the circle with one as the ground of the other, Heidegger argues that this circle is irreducible. Instead of making one the foundation of the other, he steps outside the pair to think about how they belong together. Reality must have a sayable structure and language must respond to this in order to express it, but what enables us to perceive this structure and arrive at appropriate terms? 'If speech as listening to language lets itself be told the saying, such letting can be given only insofar—and in so near—as our own essence is granted entry into the saying. We hear it only because we belong to it' (411). We can only hear and say what the world says if we are creatures capable of articulating reality and reality is articulatable, combining into what he calls the rift-design, 'the well-joined structure of a showing in which what is addressed enjoins the speakers and their speech' (408). Now we must turn to this deepest enabling condition.

III. SECTION III

We only encounter beings linguistically, but language is a response to this encounter. Heidegger steps outside of this chicken-and-egg paradox of priority to portray them as equiprimordial. Instead of asking which accounts for the other, he inquires into the way they belong together. How is it that language and beings accommodate each other, finding the other fitting or 'well-joined'? Heidegger calls the occurrence of their presencing to each other '*Ereignis*', translated here as 'propriation'. This rich word means 'event', but it also resonates with '*eigen*' which signifies what is one's own, proper, or authentic; the prefix 'er-' adds the sense of drawing something into this condition. The term also suggests '*eräugen*' and '*ereugen*', bringing something within hearing or seeing. *Ereignis* means both our being drawn into the clearing where we can perceive, think, and talk about beings, and the correlative drawing of beings into the clearing where they can appear to us. We can only speak by listening, and we can only listen if we belong to the realm of speakable things.[311] Our belonging here is complemented or 'well-joined' by Being's owning us.

After establishing our dependence on beings showing themselves, this section explores the question, 'whence does the showing arise?' (414). But Heidegger immediately chastises this inquiry: 'our question asks too much, and too quickly. . . . We can never try to know it, much less cognize it in the appropriate way . . . . We can only name it, because it will deign no discussion' (414). Once we think of the appearance to each other of beings and speech as an event, we naturally want to know why and how it happened. But we cannot look 'behind' the appearance of beings for the source or cause of their appearing, nor can we study how manifestation occurs, because any kind of examination or analysis must always already take place within the manifestation of beings (423). This primordial 'event' is not a cause which effects the clearing, nor is it an occurrence that literally took place at a specific time and place 'for it is the place that encompasses all locales and time-play-spaces'.[312] Propriation is nothing beyond the presence of speakable beings around us, just as Being or the 'there is' is not another being behind or underneath all beings.

Like language, this unique event needs to be approached on its own terms: 'there is nothing else to which propriation reverts, nothing in terms of which it might even be explained . . . . What propriates is propriation itself—and nothing besides. . . . The propriation that rules in the saying is something we can name only if we say: It—propriation—owns.'[313] In German this last phrase is closer to 'propriation propriates', resembling other tautological expressions Heidegger is fond of, such as 'the world worlds', 'the thing things', or 'language speaks' (again, clearer in German: *die Sprache spricht*). Propriation is and is only the event of our ability to perceive, think, and speak about beings, their intelligible presence to us. This event cannot be explained by reference to a cause like Forms or God or transcendental subjectivity, since these are just present beings as well, even if they possess unusual forms of presence. Like the brute fact that beings are not nothing in 'What Is Metaphysics?' (110), or the ineradicable concealment that accompanies unconcealment in 'On the Essence of Truth' (135–6), or inexplicable earth in 'The Origin of the Work of Art' (172), the event of beings and man manifesting themselves to each other must simply be experienced and noted in sober awe. Explanations fail and, in the attempt, dissipate the grateful wonder we should have.

As the source of our way of thinking, propriation cannot be accounted for by this thinking. Like language, we cannot get outside of it in order to survey it comprehensively (423). Each era gets 'sent' or appropriated into its own understanding of Being which forms a coherent way to think about everything and which determines every attempt to make sense of things. The world we live in is ruled by a 'gentle law' or 'gathered' by a coherent sense of how things are (416). We cannot use this sense of things to explain propriation because any such attempt has to employ the particular understanding that 'propriation bestows' (416) upon us.

Propriation bestows upon us a meaningful clearing in which an articulated world appears and appeals to us to articulate it. Since our essence is to be the beings to whom beings appear and who speak of these beings, propriation is what allows us to become who we are.[314] Poets and thinkers do this with excellence in that they articulate the profound folds of the world without ever taking this ability for granted or turning language into an inconspicuous medium to satisfy our desires.[315] Their articulations thankfully celebrate their ability to articulate.[316] Correlatively, beings have a 'drive' towards manifestation, so to speak, so that speaking of them brings their unconcealment to its highest point: 'the saying that rests on propriation is, as showing, the most proper mode of propriating' (420). We are, in an almost Hegelian sense, 'needed' and 'used' by the world to manifest itself more fully.[317] In this way, the event of mutual appropriation allows man and beings to bring each other to fulfillment.

Heidegger has twice intimated that our sense of a way to language would change along the way of thinking about it.[318] Rather than a mere passage to something which then gets abandoned and forgotten upon arriving at the destination, he says that 'in language as the saying, something like a way unfolds essentially'.[319] Language remains a way in that its 'gentle law' makes its way ('*wëgen*') in the world, articulating a coherent sense of things that lays out the ways of living open to us. This rift-design carves into beings as a whole the taxonomy of reality that appears self-evident to us, encompassing what is noble and what base, what is great and what mean.[320] As the farmer rends the earth to make it hospitable to his plants, so propriation has rendered the earth inhabitable for us to dwell in by depositing meaning and significance into a sayable articulation of things. It is up to us to listen to it.

We find ourselves in a world with regular intelligible patterns and graspable groups, presented with life-paths such as work, family, and friends that appeal to us and allow us to be at home on this earth. It is perfectly possible that either of these conditions could have been missing, leading to skepticism or nihilism respectively. Although this always runs the risk of hypostasizing Being into a benevolent agent, Being functions as a farmer that has broken up the world into grooves or furrows we can follow, in which meaning blooms. We may not need a way to language in the sense of an initial approach to it, but we always need the linguistic ways of the world.

STUDY QUESTIONS

1 What does it mean to bring language as language to language? Does Heidegger accomplish this? Why or why not?

2 Explain Heidegger's claim that language speaks and man only responds. Do you find this plausible? Why or why not?

i. The End of Philosophy and the Task of Thinking

This is one of Heidegger's last writings, and one of his clearest. It gives us a small sample of the dialogues with previous thinkers that occupies so much of his work but gets underrepresented in this anthology (see BW x). Like many continental thinkers, Heidegger believes that doing philosophy cannot be separated from studying the history of philosophy. Because our thought is at least partially conditioned and provoked by what precedes us, a thorough analysis of an issue should include an examination of how it has been dealt with in the past, tracing how and why we have inherited it in this particular form. Although quite brief, this essay's discussions of Hegel and Husserl supply at least a sense of this very important theme in Heidegger's writings.

Let's start with the title: from the outset, 'The End of Philosophy and the Task of Thinking' sets up a contrast between philosophy and thinking since the former is coming to an end while a task still remains for the latter. This distinction should alert us that 'thinking' is being used here as a technical term with a distinctive meaning rather than just entertaining thoughts or the activity studied by epistemology. The title lays out two questions to be explored: has philosophy ended or at least begun to end, and what might be the task for thinking at or after philosophy's end. The essay's two sections take up these questions in turn, as shown by their titles.[321]

I. THE END OF PHILOSOPHY

The first half of the title, 'The End of Philosophy', sounds portentous, even arrogant as Heidegger admits (436). He explains that philosophy's end does not mean that the activity has completely stopped, but rather that it has reached completion; it has achieved its end in the sense of its *telos* or goal. Specifically, it has fulfilled its original conception by dissolving into the sciences. Many philosophers might agree that science has indeed taken the place of philosophy in contemporary society, but bemoan this as a catastrophe, or at least unfortunate. Heidegger, however, calls this state 'the legitimate completion of philosophy',[322] a rather surprising attitude given his passionate devotion to the history of philosophy.

Obviously, in order to understand why Heidegger thinks philosophy is coming to an end we must understand what exactly he means by philosophy. He lays his cards on the table by defining philosophy as metaphysics in the first sentence of the first section.[323] Although this might seem like an artificially narrow definition since it ignores the other conventional branches of philosophy, Heidegger believes the metaphysical determination of what it means to be sets the guidelines for all other thinking.

Logic, ethics, aesthetics, and epistemology all derive from one's basic understanding of beings, making metaphysics truly the queen of philosophy.

Since he defines philosophy as metaphysics, we must now examine what he means by metaphysics, and this explanation takes up the rest of the paragraph. Metaphysics thinks 'beings as a whole ... with respect to Being' as the ground of all that is, which means 'that from which beings as such are what they are'.[324] Metaphysical theories are ways of accounting for reality by means of a single principle; things *are* by virtue of being a certain kind of thing (like substance) or by possessing a particular quality (like participation in the Forms or having been created by God), which constitutes their ground. In one astonishing sentence, Heidegger surveys a number of nineteenth-century philosophical systems in terms of the ground they assign to beings as a whole: ontic causality (perhaps Reid or Mill), Kant's transcendental subjectivity, Hegel's dialectical absolute spirit, Marx's means of production, and Nietzsche's will to power (432). Each of these philosophies contains a version of the statement, 'everything is *really* _____', where what fills in the blank explains all that is.

Now if philosophy is understood here as the attempt to discover what beings really are, then the idea that science has taken over this job stops seeming so strange. Physics has assumed the role of determining reality's basic explanatory principles, i.e., the ground or Being of beings. Philosophers have been trying to explain what makes beings real and what makes them what they are since Thales' first proposal that everything is water. Little by little, over the course of the centuries, other disciplines have taken over various sub-fields of beings (what Husserl called ontological regions) – inanimate moving objects, stars, living beings, the mind, information, etc. Whenever a type of being became amenable to mathematical analysis and experimentation for greater control, science annexed it.[325] Now, Heidegger is saying, this process is complete. Metaphysics has succeeded by becoming physics. Since this has been philosophy's intrinsic goal from inception, its present dissolution into the sciences represents its fulfillment rather than an externally imposed or accidental finish.[326]

Now this does not mean that science and philosophy are identical. Heidegger briefly recaps an argument he often makes that the sciences unwittingly depend on philosophy for the categories that define their regions of beings.[327] Scientific disciplines operate within carefully delineated boundaries: physics measures the position and velocity of particles but brackets their aesthetic appeal or mythological resonance; evolutionary biology studies fossils and skeletons but cannot accommodate the possible influence of supernatural entities. Science's success partially results from narrowing its focus to one set of beings or one aspect of them, and it only functions within that region; asking about the region itself requires a perspective external to that discipline. As soon as it begins to seriously investigate its grounding concepts, such as when scientific revolutions throw basic notions into doubt and force fundamental questions like 'what is matter?' 'what is time?', science exceeds its boundaries to step into philosophy.

II. THE TASK OF THINKING

This essay operates on an astonishing scale. Heidegger is trying to encompass the entire history of philosophy from Plato to Nietzsche and, by grasping it as a whole, to catch a glimpse of its conceptual and chronological limitations. Thinking of philosophy as a circumscribed historical movement rather than a set of timeless issues or a permanent impulse in human nature leads us towards what might lie outside its boundaries. There may be other ways to carry on the activity initiated by the Pre-Socratics besides the metaphysical project of grounding and explaining beings that Plato and Aristotle set us on. Heidegger's 'destruction' of the tradition dismantles the history of philosophy in order to understand its motivations and to uncover neglected alternatives, placing it close to genealogy as Nietzsche and Foucault practice it. The initial 'task for thinking', then, is to survey the history of philosophy for paths not taken because these possibilities may be viable options after the 'end of philosophy'. We should also examine what lies outside philosophy as metaphysics, such as the Pre-Socratic writings. Precisely because they were *pre*-philosophical, the Pre-Socratics offer hints of what a fundamentally different kind of project might look like, though it would be *post*-philosophical for us.

Thinking is not so much *non*-philosophy as *post*-philosophy, which indicates an important relationship with philosophy. Heidegger believes that throughout its history, philosophy has depended upon something which it cannot think.[328] What has been systematically omitted, what in some sense could not have been said, represents the explicit doctrines' necessary presuppositions and so leaves traces in what has been said.[329] Philosophers' omissions point towards it, kind of like how the shape of a missing puzzle piece is outlined by its very absence. As we have seen, the sciences rest upon philosophy's regional ontologies without being able to examine them; philosophy in turn presupposes this unthought which it cannot think. Out task is to find what philosophy leaves unspoken by listening very carefully to what philosophy does say.[330]

Heidegger focuses on two recent German philosophers who wielded a particularly strong influence on him. He credits Hegel with the first truly philosophical understanding of history,[331] while Husserl's *Logical Investigations* helped draw the young Heidegger into philosophy,[332] to become Husserl's prize pupil. Both philosophers also call their enterprise 'phenomenology' and proclaim the motto, 'to the things themselves' (437). All metaphysics and science aspire to this goal of an unprejudiced study of reality as it really is (see 94). Although Husserl uses the motto to criticize a specific philosophical movement,[333] it captures a universal ambition. All philosophers want to get to 'the things themselves (or the matter [*Sache*] itself)'; they just disagree on what these things are and how they can be reached. For instance, Plato bypasses the *ersatz* things of the temporal, corporeal world in favour of the really real Forms, while Nietzsche gets to what he sees as the things themselves by ignoring dysfunctional fantasies of timeless being in favour of the ever-changing forces of this world. Although they reach diametrically opposed ontologies, both thinkers seek the same formal goal of attaining the things themselves.

This motto obscures something 'precisely where philosophy has brought its matter to absolute knowledge and to ultimate evidence' (441). Even such a formal and seemingly uncontroversial statement of their subject matter unintentionally traces the silhouette of what these thinkers do not and cannot address. In fact, this unsaid operates even where they stake out their most secure epistemological positions, i.e., just where they believe they have rid themselves of all unexamined assumptions, namely, Hegel's absolute knowledge and Husserl's ultimate evidence or 'originary intuition' (443). It strikes precisely where they consider themselves least vulnerable because even their optimal evidence needs something which does not itself come to evidence.

This hidden assumption of all philosophy turns out to be, unsurprisingly, the clearing. Both Hegel and Husserl seek absolute indisputable evidence; they are looking for the state in which phenomena show themselves as they really are so that the foundations for genuine and final knowledge can be laid there. They survey various types of awareness and ways that phenomena show themselves, looking for a completely trustworthy path 'to the things themselves'. But in order to examine these types of presentations, this variety of views on the world must offer itself for inspection. Furthermore, a particular criterion of truth must appeal to them as being the correct evaluative tool, and the ambition to find absolute knowledge or evidence must strike them as the essential goal. Of course, all this is done by means of reasoning, but these reasons must appear as persuasive, something which cannot be rationally established. The way it shows itself to us is the sole 'binding character' (445) that any idea can have.

Both philosophers unknowingly presuppose that beings show themselves[334] to them in what Heidegger calls the open clearing, and that they show up in particular ways. Philosophy never thinks of the clearing but must reside within it in order to philosophize at all.[335] To deal with beings in any way one must be open to them, letting them show themselves as to-be-dealt-with in specific ways. All attempts to think about the clearing, to establish how and why we encounter beings, have misfired by referring the issue to particular beings that ground beings as a whole (Forms, God, transcendental subjectivity, etc.). Explaining Being in terms of beings is the fundamental 'ontotheological' mistake that makes all philosophy up to now metaphysics.[336] The clearing is to philosophy what philosophical regional concepts are to science, namely, that which it requires but is constitutionally incapable of thinking.

Both Hegel and Husserl consider subjectivity to be the matter of philosophy, i.e., the topic we most need to think about. For both, things themselves only appear in their appropriate form when appropriately linked to subjectivity, conceived respectively as the dialectical-historical arrival at Spirit (*Geist*) and the revelation of transcendental subjectivity by phenomenological bracketing. By founding our access to reality upon subjectivity, these philosophers attribute the establishment of our awareness of the world to our own mind; the light of reason shines out to illuminate reality. But, extending the metaphor, this overlooks the necessary condition for illumination, namely, an open space.[337] There must be a clearing, based on the metaphor of an open area in a forest where the trees thin out to let light stream in, for light to illuminate anything.

Although philosophy requires the clearing, it necessarily neglects or even obscures it, creating what Heidegger calls the forgetfulness of Being. In keeping with his frequent claim that concealing is inextricably intertwined with unconcealing, Heidegger argues that the very nature of metaphysics as the examination of beings as a whole necessarily bars us from thinking Being. 'Presence as such, and together with it the clearing that grants it, remains unheeded[.] Only what *alētheia* as clearing grants is experienced and thought, not what it is as such.'[338] To put it formulaically: both our normal focus on beings and the metaphysical inquiry into their Being obscures Being itself. We spend our everyday lives dealing with various entities – alarm clocks, cars, taxes, police officers – while a select few disengage from this busyness to metaphysically investigate how these beings are, but none of us attend to the fundamental fact that they *are*. We pay attention to what is present and its manner of presentation, but not to its presence, to the utterly simple fact that we are open to it. Ironically, the apparently innocuous pursuit of 'the things or beings themselves' is precisely the problem since focusing on beings bypasses Being or their unconcealment (truth). Heidegger says at one point that ever since *Being and Time*, his 'thinking has been concerned constantly with one occurrence: that in the history of Western thinking, right from the beginning, beings have been thought in regard to being, but the truth of being has remained unthought'.[339]

This covering over is quite natural; as Heidegger likes to translate Heraclitus, Being loves to hide (IM 120–1). Being has to withdraw for us to deal effectively with the particular beings in front of us. Light only renders objects visible if it is invisible itself; seeing the light would block our perceptions of the things that are lit, like blocks of amber separating us from the object. Just as light reveals by remaining concealed, so Being withdraws from explicit awareness to let beings present themselves. Pursuing our various endeavors, we ignore the clearing in favour of the cleared, overlooking their presencing for what is present.

Metaphysicians disengage (*epochē*) from these mundane dealings with the proliferation of individual beings in order to inquire about beings as a whole or beings qua beings.[340] They answer the question 'what are beings?' by referring beings as a whole to a ground or by determining the qualities that make things exist. The particular answers they arrive at express their era's understanding of Being but, like Hegel's forgetful Consciousness, each metaphysician takes his own answer as the final definitive word on the matter. They regard the history of metaphysical systems up to them as a series of unfortunate fumblings around in the dark, while reality waited patiently to be seen it as it really is once a clear-eyed view of things is finally won. The only value earlier philosophers have lies in how they have prepared the ground for the correct view to emerge.

Thinking studies the history of philosophy in order 'to think the historicity of that which grants a possible history to philosophy' (436). Thinking engages earlier periods in serious dialogue, eschewing questions of correctness or how closely they approximate our contemporary views or lead up to us.[341] The various metaphysical theories of beingness are ways that beings have manifested themselves to man and, collectively, they show how Being has sent many radically different understandings of Being. Since we are not in control of our understanding, a new one can occur to us at any point, rendering the notion of a final correct explanation of reality impossible. Instead of seeking final answers, we need to remain resolutely open to however things manifest themselves, committed to a 'readiness to be astounded' (327). This attitude also releases the grip of scientism, the idea that science alone tells us the truth about reality.[342]

Heidegger takes a novel approach to metaphysical questions like, 'what are beings?' or 'what is being?' or 'why are there beings at all rather than nothing?' As the first paragraph of this essay explains, 'if the answer could be given it would consist in a transformation of thinking, not in a propositional statement about a matter at stake' (431). Instead of seeking an answer, these questions highlight the mysterious fact that beings are present to us, which usually gets ignored. The fact that there is Being, or 'the belonging together of Being and thinking' (445) is the ultimate mystery, one which does not and should not seek resolution. Whereas metaphysical explanations cover it up, questioning makes it vividly manifest.

This grateful wondering at presencing is the Task of Thinking. Whereas philosophy goes 'to the matter [*Sache*] itself', thinking pursues the '"primal matter' [*Ursache*]', in order 'to become explicitly aware of the matter here called clearing' (442). Thinking aims at that which underlies all phenomena and evidence to thankfully celebrate it instead of taking credit for them and selecting among them. It is humbler than philosophy in that it ascribes to Being much that has traditionally been attributed to us, and in the simplicity of its subject matter (436). We should thoughtfully dwell in the place where we always already are but do not heed, to attend to the matter of thinking as a farmer tends her crops.

Plato took the wrong approach in trying to define Being. Of course, this is not Plato's fault since, like all thinkers, he only responded to what was revealed to him,[343] but it started philosophy down the path of metaphysics. However, studying the history of philosophy reveals its boundaries, and boundaries imply an outside. We gain some insight into what our options after the end of philosophy might be by examining what occurred before the beginning (444). Heidegger's stance on the Pre-Socratics as the only 'thinkers' in history is ambivalent. Sometimes he explicitly disavows any attempt to replicate their thought or learn directly from them since our situation is so different from theirs. Our epoch must respond to the present technological sending of Being. On this view, the Pre-Socratics only supply an instructive example of what one alternative to philosophy looks like, which can serve the genealogical function of loosening the grip of metaphysics' self-evidence, but which cannot be taken up as our own.

At other times, however, the very simplicity and ubiquity of the matter of thought, i.e., the clearing, makes it look like an ahistorical constant that anyone at any time could perceive in roughly the same way, despite Heidegger's emphasis on historicity. If it is just a matter of wondering at the fact of presencing then, even though the specific manner differs from epoch to epoch, all periods rest upon and thus could discover the mere fact of presencing. As the ahistorical basis for history, the clearing seems to be trans-epochal even though this contradicts the general thrust of his later work.[344]

Heidegger's examination of the history of philosophy in this essay reaches three conclusions:

1   Despite its apparent diversity, philosophy has been surprisingly singular in its metaphysical aspiration to think beings with respect to their Being. Every great philosopher has followed Thales' lead in offering a version of the metaphysical 'everything is really _____' statement. This metaphysical project is what makes science the successor to philosophy.

2   The genealogical element in this excavation or, more literally, de-construction (*Ab-bau*), removes the air of inevitability that has accrued to philosophy's subject matter and method due to its long tenure. Heidegger wants to expose other possibilities, a pressing need given the fact that philosophy is now drawing to a close (though sometimes he speculates that this end may last quite a long time). He is determining what philosophy is in order to see *what it is not*, i.e., what other ways of thinking might be available to us once we emerge from the long dominance of metaphysics. And the best place to look for extra-philosophical options for after the end is at the other end of philosophy, namely, before its beginning.[345] Philosophy has been one type of activity – metaphysics, i.e., the determining of universal traits of all beings, i.e., the Being of beings or beingness. Thinking this way is a historical event which began with Plato and Aristotle and is now ending as science takes over this task.

3   There is a non-philosophical activity practiced by at least some of the Pre-Socratics which does not offer another 'Everything is really _____' statement. Rather than asking about beings and their beingness, this thinking tries to 'question as to how there can be presence as such' (447). Of course, as pointed out in the very first paragraph of the essay, 'answers' to this endeavour will not take the form of a propositional fact which could only be another ground. Instead, thinking induces a 'transformation in thinking', instilling the fundamental mood or attunement of grateful wonder towards presencing rather than explaining and controlling present entities. This is the task of thinking which can only come

about with the end of philosophy. If this new way of thinking is to be genuinely different from what has come before, then we cannot predict anything about it but can only prepare ourselves for a new calling.[346]

STUDY QUESTIONS

1   How does Heidegger define philosophy? Why? Is this a fair characterization? Why or why not? How does he define thinking?
2   In what way(s) is this essay genealogical?

CHAPTER 4

RECEPTION AND INFLUENCE

Heidegger is unquestionably one of the most influential philoso-phers of the twentieth century, quite possibly the single most important figure in the continental tradition. I have argued at some length in *A Thing of This World* (Braver, 2007) that he stands to the twentieth century the way Kant stood to the nine-teenth, as the unavoidable thinker who must be dealt with one way or another by everyone in his wake, and the figure to whom much of what follows can be traced. Virtually every important continental philosopher of the century pays homage to his genius, even those strongly opposed to him.

His early work created existential phenomenology by fusing Husserl's methods with Kierkegaard's concerns (along with Kant's transcendental strategy and Dilthey's hermeneutics). This movement was central to continental philosophy in the first half of the twentieth century, lead by Jean-Paul Sartre (whose *Being and Nothingness* has been jokingly called a French 'translation' of *Being and Time*), and Maurice Merleau-Ponty, whose *Phe-nomenology of Perception* fills in gaps on the body and perception left by *Being and Time*.

After the *Kehre* or change in his thought in the early-thirties, Heidegger left existential phenomenology behind, issuing a decisive critique of Sartre in the 'Letter on Humanism'. His later work tries to forge a profoundly new way of thinking; it is far more innovative (and more difficult) than the early work, and it has enjoyed even greater influence. The group of thinkers loosely grouped together as postmodernists all work in the shadow of the later thought, while the Frankfurt school partially defines itself in opposition to Heidegger. On the other hand, while his early work has been somewhat assimilated and accepted by ana-lytic philosophers, especially in the field of philosophy of mind, the later work remains the unread subject of easy attack or ridicule in analytic circles. Its 'poetic' or 'mystical' style, as well as its intense focus on history, could not but have alienated many analytic thinkers. I will briefly discuss three prominent continental thinkers who owe an especially large debt to Heidegger's later thought.

Hans-Georg Gadamer was the twentieth century's leader of hermeneutic philosophy, a movement going back to Schleiermacher's work in the early nineteenth century which reached an important turning point and expansion in *Being and Time*. A personal student of Heidegger ('what was most important for me, however, I learned from Heidegger'[1]), Gadamer combines ideas from the early work, in particular the notion of the fore-structures of understanding, with much from the later work, especially Heidegger's discussions of truth, history, and art. Gadamer traces his own foundational idea that artworks have a distinct kind of truth to Heidegger's talk, 'The Origin of the Work of Art',[2] and Gadamer's view of texts as embodying their period's world-view, forcing us to understand them on their own terms instead of blithely translating them into ours, reflects both Heidegger's claims and his practice in the later work.

Michel Foucault said in one of his last interviews that 'Heidegger has always been for me the essential philosopher . . .. My whole philosophical development was determined by my reading of Heidegger'.[3] Foucault divides history into epochs, each with its own system of truth that determines what kind of statements and scientific approaches are allowable, which is why he singles out Heidegger's historical conception of truth as particularly important.[4] Although this notion develops throughout Foucault's career – from the *episteme* to a disciplinary apparatus to games of truth – it retains a basic similarity to Heidegger's epochal understandings of Being.[5]

Jacques Derrida, perhaps the most brilliant continental philosopher since Heidegger, calls Heidegger 'uncircumventable',[6] noting that his own work 'would not have been possible without the opening of Heidegger's questions'.[7] Derrida insists 'that Heidegger's text is extremely important to me, and that it constitutes a novel, irreversible advance all of whose critical resources we are far from having exploited' (Ibid., 54). Even his famous term 'deconstruction' was partially inspired by Heidegger's early '*Destruktion*' of the tradition. In addition to Heidegger's willingness to give 'violent' readings of philosophical texts,

Derrida continues Heidegger's struggle with the problem of how to escape from metaphysics.

How Heidegger's reputation will fare in the future is, of course, impossible to tell. For those who approach the study of philosophy historically, Heidegger's broad influence makes him unavoidable. The fact that he has continued to publish prolifically even decades after his death ensures that there will continue to be work to be done in Heidegger scholarship for some time to come. I certainly believe that he hit on a number of crucial insights and raised many profound questions, whose depths we are far from plumbing. One of the most fascinating features of his thought is that his absolute focus on the single topic of Being is balanced by or, rather, carried out through the exploration of an astounding variety of subjects. This is only fitting since thinking, considered as a whole, is and can only be the expression of Being.

NOTES

CHAPTER 1

1 Unless otherwise noted, all references in this book are to *Basic Writings*.
2 'Patience is the truly *human* way of being thoughtful about things. Genuine patience is one of the basic virtues of philosophizing – virtue which understands that we always have to build up the pile of kindling with properly selected wood so that it may at one point catch fire' (HPS 73).
3 Quoted in Biemel (1976: 6). See also STF 5.
4 See 77, BP 72–73, BP 155, PIK 48, PIK 136, PIK 252, PIK 289, KPM 141–142. Many critics have discussed this point, with Sherover (1972) and Blattner (1999) addressing it at length (see Braver (2007: 532n 9) for a full list of references).
5 See TB 28, TB 46, N 4:141, FS 40–41, M 125, M 187.
6 I will often retain Heidegger's term 'man' despite its sexism because it acts as a technical term in his usage.
7 See 238, 276, 281.

CHAPTER 2

1 See 238–9, 264, 281, WCT 50, N I:36, STF 85, M 267, EGT 56, OBT 159.
2 See 58, 234, 246, 263, 415, WCT 98, WCT 110, WCT 152, WCT 202, WCT 239, PR 5, N III:56, OBT 193, OBT 198, BQ 159, P 149.
3 See 234, 263, BP 16, BP 68, BP 75, BP 275, BP 293, BP 299, BT 189/149, BT 213/169, BT 414/362.
4 PIK 16–17, see also BW 44–6, BW 54, BW 160, BW 275–7, HCT 143–4, FCM 357.
5 PIK 16, see also BW 289, BP 72, KPM 7, KPM 50, KPM 159.
6 See 276, KPM 158.
7 See 59, 66. Although the stated goal of the book is to find the right horizon for the meaning of Being, to which the analysis of Dasein's Being is subordinated (see 60–2, 86–7, BT 278/235, KPM 198–9), this topic was to have been addressed primarily in the Third Division of Part One which never got published. The two divisions we have

focus on explaining Dasein's way of Being, i.e., the existential analysis (see 55).

8   BP 78, see also BW 44, PR 63.
9   PM 287, see also PM 232, BW 126, BW 242, BW 432, M 186, M 317, ID 70, OBT 99, OBT 133.
10 This strain of his work is underrepresented in this anthology, as Krell admits at BW x. The most relevant essays are 'Modern Science, Metaphysics, and Mathematics' and 'The End of Philosophy and the Task of Thinking'.
11 Heidegger's history of Being is not entirely consistent across his career. The Pre-Socratics, who seem to have anticipated much of Heidegger's own thought, might count as a separate era, though he generally exempts them from the ranks of metaphysics entirely. It is also unclear to what extent the contemporary era of technological standing-reserve is distinct from the modern age of substance.
12 See 291–3, 432–3, STF 138, OBT 58.
13 See 232, 446–7, M 269, M 317, WCT 100, BQ 170, PM 104n. a, PM 277. STF 64, CP 121/§85, N III:217, OBT 193, OBT 196.
14 FS 22, see also FS 59–60, TB 6, M 322, M 333, PR 62.
15 See 201, 288, 436, PR 79, PR 105, ID 66–7, N III:164, FS 61.
16 See TB 41, N III:189–90, M 146, WT 39–40.
17 See 436, WCT 159–60, M 302.
18 Although his early work does not follow this principle, the introduction to *Being and Time* does state it in the discussion of the history of philosophy (71). Also, the book's final sentence puts its opening thesis into question (see also TB 28).
19 BQ 150–1, see also BW 103, BW 190.
20 See 241, BQ 146, WT 242, PM 319, OWL 85, OWL 93, PLT 190.

CHAPTER 3

1   See 55–7, 385, FCM 9.
2   See 94, PIA 48, PIA 85.
3   See 51–2, 187, 291–2.
4   We can see a parallel here with the pre-ontological understanding of Being one must possess just to ask the question of Being (see 45–6), as well as the necessary circle between studying artworks in order to grasp art relying on a previous understanding of what art is in order to pick out artworks to study (144).
5   Sartre, heavily influenced by 'What is Metaphysics?', adapts this argument to show the 'reality' of nothingness in human consciousness in *Being and Nothingness*.
6   Years later, Heidegger remarked that 'the intention of the lecture, held before a gathering of scientists and faculty, was thus: to show the scientists that there is something other than the object of their exclusive occupations and that this other precisely first enables that very thing with which they are preoccupied' (FS 57). He defends it against the charge of being 'arbitrary and contrived' by attributing

the formulation to Taine, 'who may be taken as the representative and sign of an entire era' (PM 84n. a).

7 Carnap (1959: 69–72).

8 98, see also 129.

9 98, see also 45.

10 See 53, 73, 151, BT 176/137, PIA 17.

11 97, see also BT 166–7/129. Heidegger's unabashed call to end the hegemony of logic particularly upsets Carnap: 'the author of the treatise is clearly aware of the conflict between his questions and statements, and logic . . ... All the worse for logic!' Carnap (1959: 71).

12 100, see also BT 175/136, HCT 256, N I:99, FCM 67, FCM 89.

13 N I:51, see also WIP 91, FCM 68.

14 See 105, 108, OTB 199.

15 Since it has given rise to so much virulent misunderstanding, I will repeat that Heidegger is not attacking or dismissing reason, but trying to view it as one faculty among many. Each has its strengths and weaknesses, but philosophy has only praised reason and attacked emotions for virtually all of its history.

16 100, see also KPM 166.

17 Heidegger does not explicitly say that boredom reveals the nothing, but this fits his description better than revealing beings as a whole. See his more detailed discussion in FCM.

18 In the sense of *inter-esse* as being-in-the-world in a concernful way (see 371).

19 See 103, FCM 86, FCM 103.

20 See BT 180–2/141–2, BT 230–5/186–91, BT 391–4/341–4, HCT 284.

21 101, see also BT 231/186, HCT 289.

22 101, see also FCM 92, FCM 138.

23 See 58, 160.

24 See BT 99/69, BT 106/75, CP 348.

25 BT 232/187, see also BT 105/75, HCT 291. It is intriguing to speculate on how love might perform this function, though Heidegger does not explain how it happens.

26 BT 393/343, see also BT 231/187, PM 88n. a. As Bill Blattner points out in this volume's 'prequel', this description resembles depression, which Heidegger himself suffered from, rather than what we would now call anxiety (see Blattner 2006: 13, 142, 185n. 88).

27 106, see also BT 234/189.

28 Thus, in anxiety, 'Dasein finds itself *face to face* with the 'nothing' of the possible impossibility of its existence . . ... Being-towards-death is essentially anxiety' (BT 310/266, see also BT 295/251, HCT 291).

29 106, see also FCM 82.

30 102, see also FCM 147. Here we can see the possible inspiration for Sartre's notion of *de trop*.

31 See 105, M 278.

32 103, see also FS 57, BQ 150.

33 Heidegger will come to define metaphysics precisely as the making of this kind of distinction, but by then he will also have distanced himself from metaphysics thus defined. See e.g., M 339, N 2:230.

34 103, see also 190, KPM 51, KPM 166–7, PM 234.

35 Compare Sartre's famous description of Roquentin's nauseous encounter with the chestnut tree: 'the words had vanished and with them the significance of things, their methods of use, and the feeble points of reference which men have traced on their surface . . .. Usually existence hides itself . . .. And then all of a sudden, there it was, clear as day: existence had suddenly unveiled itself. It had lost the harmless look of an abstract category: it was the very paste of things' Sartre (1964: 127).

36 BP 159, see also BP 301, BT 155/119, HCT 244.

37 BT 416/364, see also BP 171, HCT 202.

38 102, see also KPM 199–200.

39 100, see also 94, 104.

40 101, see also BT 321/277, BT 394/343, FCM 283.

41 FCM 143, italics in original, see also FCM 127.

42 FCM 171, italics added, see also FCM 165.

43 Heidegger often describes his early work as continuing and radicalizing Kant's transcendental inquiry. Where Kant examined the conditions for the possibility of specific types of judgments – scientific, ethical, and aesthetic – Heidegger analyzes our openness to the world, i.e., our being Da-sein or the clearing, as the condition for the possibility of any kind of experience whatsoever (see PIK 289, PIK 292). In 'What Is Metaphysics?' he seems to waver between the claim that an experience of the nothing is itself the enabling condition of all awareness (see 104, 108, 109, KPM 50–1, KPM 167, KPM 199, FS 57) and the claim that anxiety simply allows us to explicitly experience the openness that we are always already within (see 110, FCM 143). Personally, I favour the latter view. There is also the suggestion of a compromise between these two options in the idea that anxiety is 'constant though doubtlessly obscured . . . only sleeping' (105–6, see also BT 234/189, BT 299/255, HCT 290) but this notion seems phenomenologically dubious to me.

44 See 109, PM 233–4.

45 As has been often noted, Heideggerian wonder is similar to Wittgenstein's early definition of mysticism: 'it is not *how* things are in the world that is mystical, but *that* it exists' Wittgenstein (1988: 73/§6.44). Wittgenstein later describes the feeling he associates with the idea of an absolute good in similar terms: 'I believe the best way of describing it is to say that when I have it *I wonder at the existence of the world*. And I am then inclined to use such phrases as "how extraordinary that anything should exist"' Wittgenstein (1993: 41).

46 Such as grateful thinking (*denken/danken*) or preserving/sheltering the mystery, notions we will be examining in other chapters.

47 See 238, FS 57.

48 See 138, 431, IM 32, WIP 97.
49 IM 30–1, see also BQ 146, BQ 150–1, FCM 172.
50 See 110, KPM 1, OWL 25.
51 109, see also KPM 170.
52 See 57, 110, WCT 142, FCM 283.
53 This kind of 'apprenticeship' in thinking also occurs in the first section of 'The Origin of the Work of Art'. See 144, 379.
54 Repeated for other topics at 45, 98, 144, 276–7, ET 113, OWL 71.
55 See 118, 162, 175, MFL 2, MFL 124, BQ 14–18, BT 257/214.
56 See BT 257–8/214–15, BQ 31.
57 MFL 125, see also BT 258/215, BQ 20.
58 See 115, 175, 312, BQ 44–5.
59 In official phenomenological terms, it is 'intentional' in that it is directed towards an object.
60 BQ 18, see also BQ 82, BQ 174, BP 210, HPS 65, MFL 127, MFL 216–17, PM 280, FCM 342.
61 122, see also 176–7, 446, BT 263/220, BQ 82, PIS 350, ET 9, ET 86, MFL 127–8.
62 Nietzsche (1989a: 9).
63 123, see also FCM 339.
64 See 123, 126.
65 See 123–4. Neither Nietzsche nor Derrida subscribe to this view either, for that matter, despite caricatures.
66 125, see also 351, ET 45, P 143.
67 124, see also 178, KPM 87, KPM 198, FCM 341.
68 See STF 9, EF 93.
69 129, see also FS 8, DT 65, M 242, OBT 74.
70 See 131, 156–7, PM 144n. b, TB 35.
71 126, see also 103, 181, 442–5, BQ 175–6, BQ 181, EGT 104, EGT 120–1.
72 Note, though, that this ontological engagement still deals with beings, but now for the sake of Being or the clearing rather than fulfilling our desires. After all, Being is always the Being of a being (see 50, 186).
73 This is Heidegger's version of the phenomenological notion of intentionality, which took the form of being-in-the-world in *Being and Time*.
74 See 127, 177, FCM 339, FCM 342.
75 See 78, 121, 406, MFL 125–6, FCM 29.
76 See 127, BP 221.
77 See 98–9, 129.
78 This is Heidegger's version of Husserl's doctrine of adumbrations, the idea that the perception of a physical object necessarily perceives only part of it; the sides facing us hide the back sides. If we turn the object to see the back sides, then they now obscure the sides that had been visible.
79 BQ 127–8, see also BQ 178, EGT 118, EGT 122.
80 130, see also 178–9, 448, BP 322, KPM 197, EGT 71, EGT 114.

81 See 130, EGT 108, M 323.

82 In his marginal notes from 1943 (PM 148n. a), Heidegger points to a significant shift or 'leap' occurring between Sections Five and Six (though he does not single out this paragraph).

83 See 131. *Being and Time* calls this understanding what 'one' (*das Man*) does with things (see BT 167/129, BT 213/169, BT 264/222, BP 322).

84 We can note a significant overlap here with Emmanuel Levinas who defines knowledge as reducing the other to the same or, in Heidegger's terms, in-sistent closedness (see Levinas (1996: 14, 151)). Gadamer also discusses the dangers of prejudices, though he stresses the fact that they play a useful and ineliminable role in understanding as well.

85 See 132, 251, 262, 295–6, 331, CP §274/348–9, WCT 76–7, FS 8, PM 307, QT 104, N III:176, N IV:44, N IV:203, OBT 71, OBT 77.

86 124, see also BQ 21, N III:56.

87 135, see also EGT 26, IM 115, M 184.

88 See 135–6, 172, 204, PLT 222–3, PLT 225.

89 Although I find that his early work betrays this principle, the introduction to *Being and Time* does state it (71). Also, the book's final sentence puts its fundamental thesis into question.

90 See 138, 431, 442, M 333, WIP 97, FCM 59.

91 See 50–3, 187, 289, 435, TDP 25, BP 13, PIK 20, PIK 24–7, N II:112, N II:116.

92 See 246, 436, BQ 35, BQ 38, WCT 159–60, WCT 165.

93 Heidegger makes the same move with beings and Being at 48, the nothing at 98, and truths and the essence of truth at 116.

94 See 144, BT 195/153, BT 362/314.

95 See 156. One of the features uniting 'post-modern' thinkers such as Levinas, Derrida, and Foucault is this rallying cry to protect difference or otherness against homogenization though it takes quite different forms in their works.

96 As early as the supplement to his dissertation, Heidegger insisted that 'a basic requirement for a theory of categories is *characterizing and demarcating the different domains of objects into spheres that are categorially irreducible to one another*' (Sup 63, see also Sup 78, BW 58, BW 66).

97 A few years earlier in talking about the history of philosophy, he said that 'the basic presupposition for being able to take the past seriously lies in willing not to make one's own labour easier than did those who are supposed to be revived' (BP 100).

98 144, see also 379–80.

99 Nietzsche made the same point about how language distinguishes an agent from her actions, all the way up to the ultimate subject: 'we find ourselves in the midst of a rude fetishism when we call to mind the basic presuppositions of the metaphysics of language – which is to say, of *reason*. It is *this* which sees everywhere deed and doer . . . and which *projects* its belief in the ego-substance on

to all things – only thus does it *create* the concept 'thing'. . . . I fear
we are not getting rid of God because we still believe in grammar'
Nietzsche (1990: 48).

100 150, see also 125, 258, 353, WCT 233, FCM 23.
101 151–2, see also 408, BT 207/164, IPR 6, TDP 71–2, PIS 288,
     HCT 266, BP 208–9, EGT 64–6.
102 See 46, 65–6, 148, HCT 129.
103 See 66, 157, 165, 194, Sup 160, BP 22–3, BP 117, HCT 29, HCT
     87, HCT 136, HCT 300, WT 39–40, ET 197.
104 See 148, 150, 153, 156.
105 See BT 99/69, CP §274/348.
106 See BT 106/75, BT 412–5/361–4. The situation is actually more
     complicated than this, with a middle phase when you are improv-
     ing a skill or repairing a broken tool (see BT 201/158).
107 161, see also 195.
108 164, see also N I:187.
109 See 100, confirmed here at 151.
110 See 164–5. *Being and Time* uses the term 'Dasein' instead of 'man'
     or 'consciousness' to avoid this problem.
111 Wittgenstein's early conception of language centers around his
     picture theory of meaning which takes this similarity as
     fundamental.
112 See 162, 118, 176, 446.
113 See 162, 181, PLT 197. The art historian Meyer Schapiro criti-
     cized Heidegger for attributing the shoes in Van Gogh's painting
     to a peasant farmer when they were in fact Van Gogh's own shoes.
     However, we can see from Heidegger's rejection of artistic truth
     as correct portrayal that, regardless of its accuracy, Schapiro's
     objection misses the point. Derrida says as much in his extended
     discussion of their exchange: 'Schapirio is mistaken about the
     primary function of the pictorial reference. He also gets wrong a
     Heideggerian argument which should ruin in advance his own
     restitution of the shows to Van Gogh: art as "putting to work of
     truth" is neither an "imitation", nor a "description" copying the
     "real", nor a "reproduction" ' Derrida (1987: 312, see also 325).
114 177, see also 122, 446, BT 261–3/218–20, MFL 127–28, BQ 82,
     PIS 350, ET 9, ET 86.
115 176, see also BT 262/220.
116 This fits in with Heidegger's early view that the equipment we use
     helps constitute our identity by making up our world. 'We are
     able to understand and encounter ourselves constantly in a spe-
     cific way by way of the beings which we encounter as intraworldly.
     The shoemaker is not the shoe; but shoe-gear, belonging to the
     equipmental contexture of his environing world, is intelligible as
     the piece of equipment that it is only by way of the particular
     world that belongs to the existential constitution of the Dasein as
     being-in-the-world. In understanding itself by way of *things*, the
     Dasein understands itself as being-in-the-world by way of its

world. The shoemaker is not the shoe but, existing, he is his world' (BP 171, see also BP 159, BT 416/364).

117   EGT 26, see also EGT 99, PM 313, WCT 98, WCT 110, WCT 237, BQ 178, BQ 183.

118   178. Heidegger connects Being, the clearing, and Truth many times (see 177, 197, 210, 235, 240, BQ 183).

119   See 58, 234, 246, 263, 415, WCT 98, WCT 110, WCT 152, WCT 202, WCT 239, PR 5, N III:56, OBT 193, OBT 198, BQ 159, P 149.

120   BQ 127–8, see also EGT 100, EGT 122, P 135, P 142.

121   179, see also 185. Heidegger makes a brief argument that truth's strife between unconcealment and concealment bears an affinity with artworks' earth-world strife (187), although the two cannot simply be identified with each other (180). Art's structural isomorphism with truth is what accounts for its unusual ability to effect truth. He lists a number of other ways that truth occurs in beings (186–7), but this is one reason why artworks enjoy a privileged status.

122   See 168, 170.

123   FCM 347, see also FCM 355, BT 114/83, BT 406/355.

124   179, see also 191, 200, BQ 144, CP §5/11, CP §243/272, CP §269/339.

125   172, see also PLT 170, PLT 224.

126   See 415, DT 65. This strategy resembles Husserl's 'formal indications'.

127   See 223, PT 56, EHP 43, STF 138.

128   173, see also 135–6, 171, 189.

129   197, see also N I:119, N I:187, IM 204–5.

130   190, see also 178, P 149–50.

131   See 210, BQ 164.

132   181, italics in original, see also 206, IM 140, IM 170, N I:195, N I:198, PM 178. This synthesis can be seen as a fascinating reinterpretation of the medieval doctrine of the identity of transcendentals, i.e., the idea that the highest values that apply to all categories – Being, truth, and beauty, as well as good, one, etc. – are all the same. One of the best known formulations of this doctrine was given by Duns Scotus, the subject of Heidegger's *Habilitationschrift* (a German version of the dissertation).

133   167, see also 159–60, 361–2.

134   See 169, 193, 199, 242.

135   For a detailed discussion of this topic, see Braver (2007: 325–9).

136   Hegel, Nietzsche, and early Heidegger all use this phrase (see BT 186/145, BT 188/148).

137   See 229, 224, 248.

138   BT 67/42, quoted at 229.

139   230, see also 232.

140   225–6, see also 247.

141   224, see also FCM 42, KPM 5.

142 See 226–7, 235, 246, N III:189, N III:217, N IV:207, PM 281, M 186–7, M 268–9, CP 120/§83.

143 See M 300, M 322–3, M 375, TB 37.

144 See 234, 246, 263.

145 235, see also N IV:211–12, EGT 99, EGT 122.

146 See 235, M 347, N IV:208, STF 64.

147 See 247, PM 278, PM 288.

148 233, see also OBT 132–3, FS 59–60, M 334.

149 235. One of the obstacles here is the 'puzzling ambiguity' (233) by which Being can mean a specific way of Being or the mere presence of beings at all. Heidegger admits to his own 'ambiguous use of the word 'Being'. . . between 'Being' as 'the Being of beings,' and 'Being' as 'Being' in respect of its proper sense, that is, in respect of its truth (the clearing)' (OWL 20, see also OWL 26). He comes to refer to the latter with a number of different terms (such as *Ereignis*, Beyng, Being crossed out, and the truth of Being) to prevent this confusion.

150 Note that the term 'passive' only roughly approximates Heidegger's ideas. He actually wants to forego the entire active-passive distinction (see DT 61, BQ 151). I address this topic in great detail in 2007: 273–9.

151 BT 329/284, see also BP 221.

152 WCT 142, see also WCT 151, P 147, FS 73, PM 279, PM 294, DT 64, PR 69, PR 75, CP 167/§120.

153 N IV:152, see also N III:68.

154 See 261, 296–304, M 257–8, P 103–4, CP 179/§134, CP 221/§192, N IV:28, N IV:86, N IV:103.

155 N IV:93, see also N IV:139, PM 300.

156 FS 40–1, see also FS 47, BW 259, P 103, M 257–8, M 287.

157 KPM 165, see also BW 234, BW 240–1, BW 260, PM 135, M 276.

158 234, see also 231, 241, 252, 259.

159 232. Heidegger applies the same point to Nietzsche at 241.

160 Heidegger's many discussions of the difficulty of escaping metaphysics is one of his greatest influences on Derrida.

161 232, see also WCT 161.

162 IM 56, see also BW 314, WT 39, M 268–9, STF 171, STF 187. In a 1931 course, Heidegger discusses Aristotle's treatment of beings in terms of categories and potential-actual: 'what is the origin of this distinction? What is the justification for this twofold deployment in the address and saying of being? Aristotle offers no explanation or reason for this, neither here nor elsewhere. He does not even so much as raise the question. This differentiation of the *on* is simply put forth. It is somewhat like when we say that mammals and birds are included in the class of animals' (AM 8, see also AM 102, FCM 357). Foucault takes up this specific topic – namely, the historical origin and metaphysical arbitrariness of animal taxonomy – in *The Order of Things*.

163 See 132, 235, 242.

164 See 226, 254, M 19, M 37, PM 279, CP 120/§85.

165 M 333, see also PM 318.

166 409, see also 372, 384, WCT 6, PT 27, N IV:214, PR 47, PLT 6, PLT 181, PLT 209, PM 293, OWL 76.

167 This bears a similarity to Wittgenstein's solution to the pseudo-problem of rule-following. See Wittgenstein (2001: §198, §201, §217, §219, §506). We can also see the influence of Husserl's understanding of phenomenology as based on intuitive evidence.

168 We can see here remnants of Husserl's notion of categorial intuition which claims that we directly 'perceive' phenomena such as logical relations between objects of our experience.

169 See PR 111, PM 234, DT 83, M 73.

170 See 251, 264, PM 235.

171 PM 232, see also PM 277, PM 289.

172 Z 217, see also BW 180, BW 330, BW 361, STF 148–9, STF 154–5.

173 See 251, 262, N IV:44, N IV:202–3, BQ 159, OTB 77, PM 313, PM 319.

174 238, see also 235, 391, 415, WCT 121, N IV:217–18, TB 19, TB 38–40.

175 Here is a point on which Heidegger agrees with Nietzsche who uses the example of lightning as a phenomenon in which the subject-action distinction collapses. See Nietzsche (1989b: I.13, p. 45).

176 See 235, 248, 252, PM 283, PM 308–10, ID 30–3, DT 77–8, WCT 79, M 133, M 281.

177 229, see also 220, 233, 252, N I:193, PM 284.

178 This idea has its roots in *Being and Time*'s initial definition of Dasein as being-in-the-world, and ultimately in Husserl's notion of intentionality. It also marks another point of contact between Heidegger and Wittgenstein.

179 See 243, PM 324, EGT 14, ID 43–4.

180 See 258, Z 217.

181 See 170, 198, 228–30, Z 217, ID 31.

182 234, see also 231, 237, 246, 337, BQ 163, M 211, CP 213/§178, PR 86, WCT 121, PLT 184.

183 241, see also 330.

184 See 258, M 238, FS 80.

185 See 101–2, 227, 233–4, PM 236, CP 169/§122, PLT 228.

186 See 125, 128, 151, 333, 351–3, Z 62.

187 217, see also 262, 264, PR 96, ID 39.

188 See 230, 237, 262–3, OBT 232, FCM 291.

189 262, see also 132, 251, 331, FS 56.

190 And certain ideas found in *Being and Time*: 'resoluteness constitutes the *loyalty* of existence to its own Self. As resoluteness which is ready for *anxiety*, this loyalty is at the same time a possible way of revering the sole authority which a free existing can have' (BT 443/391).

191 See WCT 143, WCT 146, WCT 235.

192 See WCT 126, WCT 142.

193 See 233, 248, WCT 235.

194 Heidegger even uses Kuhn's key term 'paradigm' in a discussion of science a few years before this work (ET 46). Many have noted the similarities between Kuhn and continental thought, including Kuhn himself: 'the philosophy I knew and had been exposed to, and the people in my environment to talk to, were all of them out of the English logical empiricist tradition, in one way or another. This was a tradition which by and large had no use for the continental and particularly the German philosophical tradition. I think, in some sense or other, I can be described as in some part having reinvented that tradition for myself' Kuhn (2002: 321).

195 This contradicts the view of the neo-Kantian school that dominated German academic philosophy when Heidegger began his studies that the first *Critique* is a work of epistemology.

196 272, see also BT 189/149, BT 213/169, BT 414/362, HCT 145, PIK 22, N II:114, BQ 48, BQ 60, BQ 73. Nietzsche, whom Heidegger was studying intensely and beginning to lecture on at this time, also claims that interpretation is built into experience: 'against positivism, which halts at phenomena – 'there are only *facts*' – I would say: No, facts is precisely what there is not, only interpretations' Nietzsche (1968: §481).

197 See PIK 289, KPM 141–2.

198 See e.g., OBT 57, OBT 73.

199 See discussions of the similar notion of worldhood: 'the world as already unveiled in advance is such that we do not in fact specifically occupy ourselves with it, or apprehend it, but instead it is so self-evident, so much a matter of course, that we are completely oblivious of it' (BP 165).

200 Since Aristotle dominates Medieval science too, this period needs no separate discussion (281, 283).

201 275, see also 49–50, 434–5, FCM 186, KPM 7, KPM 87, OBT 59, TDP 22, PLT 170.

202 Heidegger applies this 'hermeneutic circle' argument to other topics at 45–6, 98, 144, ET 113, OWL 71.

203 Notice how close the wording is between the early: 'we live already in an understanding of Being' (44), and the later: 'the mathematical is that evident aspect of things within which we are always already moving' (277).

204 See 271, 432–3, OBT 58, BQ 47–8, IM 110–11, FS 9, M 206, AM 67.

205 Kuhn (1996: 150). Compare with Foucault: 'people have often wondered how on earth nineteenth-century botanists and biologists managed not to see the truth of Mendel's statements. But it was precisely because Mendel spoke of objects, employed methods and placed himself within a theoretical perspective totally alien to the biology of his time . . .. Here was a new object, calling

for new conceptual tools, and for fresh theoretical foundations. Mendel spoke the truth, but he was not *dans le vrai* (within the true) of contemporary biological discourse: it simply was not along such lines that objects and biological concepts were formed. A whole change in scale, the deployment of a totally new range of objects in biology was required before Mendel could enter into the true' Foucault (1972: 224).

206 See 130, 178, OBT 60, PLT 170.

207 Many of these ideas are explored in greater depth in *Being and Time*'s discussion of Descartes' scientific space (BT §19–21, pp. 123/89–134/101).

208 288, see also 201, FCM 188, FCM 261, OBT 60, OBT 131–2, PR 55, PR 79, PR 87.

209 304, see also 50–2, 187, WCT 222.

210 See 50–2, 187, BP 52–4, N II:112–13, WCT 33, WCT 151.

211 290. Kuhn also believes that early converts to a new paradigm often have to cling to it in spite of greater evidence supporting established science; see, e.g., Kuhn 1996: 150–9.

212 290. Kuhn similarly comments that 'all these natural phenomena [Galileo] saw differently from the way they had been seen before' Kuhn (1996: 119, see also 150) and Norwood Hanson gives a negative answer to the question, '*do Kepler and Tycho see the same thing in the east at dawn?*' since 'theories and interpretations are "there" in the seeing from the outset' Hanson (1958: 5, 10). According to Hanson, this is due to the fact that 'seeing is a "theory-laden" undertaking. Observation of x is shaped by prior knowledge of x' (ibid., 19, see also 54, 157). We can also see a resemblance with the Duhem-Quine thesis that, due to the fact that observation is laden with holistic theories, there is no such thing as a truly crucial experiment that forces us to abandon a theory; we can always revise assumptions or interpret observations differently instead.

213 291, see also OBT 59, BT 414/362.

214 292–3, see also 278, BT 128/95–6.

215 292, see also BT 445/393, OBT 58–9, PLT 170, FCM 32, FCM 89, FCM 186, FCM 275. What Heidegger calls the mathematical, Foucault calls an era's '*episteme*' or 'historical *a priori*' in his early work: 'this *a priori* is what, in a given period, delimits in the totality of experience a field of knowledge, defines the mode of being of the objects that appear in that field, provides man's everyday perception with theoretical powers, and defines the conditions in which he can sustain a discourse about things that is recognized to be true' Foucault (1994: 158, see also xxii).

216 296, see also 332, OBT 66, OBT 69, OBT 81, OBT 183.

217 302, see also 276, 290, 305.

218 304, see also 300, FS 8, OBT 60.

219 OBT 67, see also OBT 71, OBT 176–7, OBT 191, OBT 195, OBT 216, BW 303.

220 OBT 69, see also 295–6, 332.
221 See OBT 66, OBT 75, N IV:28, N IV:86, N IV:103, PM 300, CP §259/300.
222 See OBT 76, OBT 84. Braver (2007: 303–8) discusses this topic in greater depth.
223 313, see also 151, 361.
224 See 66, 83.
225 318, see also 184, 244.
226 See 152, BT 190–1/150, PR 47, TDP 71–5, WCT 129–30.
227 Except in the unusual circumstance of anxiety discussed in 'What Is Metaphysics?' (see 101, 359).
228 See 105, 261, 319, 372, 409, ID 35. I discuss this topic at greater length in Braver (2007: 305–25).
229 322, see also OBT 144, OTB 217, ID 34ff, WCT 135, EHP 87.
230 320, see also 352.
231 DT 50, see also 321, 326, EHP 87, BT 100/70, PM 313.
232 See 129, 153, 172, OBT 72, OBT 85, WCT 43.
233 324, see also 217, N I:46–7.
234 WCT 234, see also OTB 217, ID 34.
235 Heidegger discusses the title of this book, which he considers the place where 'the modern concept of science is coined,' at 299.
236 Descartes (1985: VI., 62, 142–3).
237 OTB 188, all italics mine, see also ID 35, OWL 62, M 152, QT 37, FS 63, FS 75, WCT 234.
238 See 327, 331.
239 332–3, see also 420, QT 36, QT 41, QT 43.
240 332, see also 295–6, ID 34, FS 56.
241 320, see also EHP 74, WCT 190–1.
242 Heidegger makes a similar case for artistic creation at 200.
243 See 130, 178, 185, EGT 71, EGT 114.
244 332, see also 335, 339, PR 79–80, PR 88, WCT 43.
245 313, see also 329, OTB 217, Z 266.
246 334, see also QT 41–3, M 56, ID 37, ID 40, DT 50.
247 See 329, N 4:196, PR xiv–xv, PR 62, TB 17.
248 QT 44, see also BW 235, BW 238, BW 391, BW 415, PM 308–10.
249 See 330, 335, QT 45, FS 9, PR 51, PR 111.
250 QT 39, see also QT 44, PR 108, BW 433, TB 52.
251 Here we can see how deeply Heidegger influenced Foucault.
252 See 133–6, 172, 223, 238, 448, EHP 43.
253 PR 91, see also TB 9.
254 337, sees also 233–4, 239, 330, 420, EGT 25, EGT 58.
255 See 234, 245, 337, QT 44–5.
256 BT 123/89148/113, see also HCT 223–36.
257 348. Heidegger often contrasts correctness with truth, see 151, 313, 331, 408.
258 348, see also 350, PLT 215–16.
259 See 221, 223, 410–11, 423, BT 205/162, PLT 192, PLT 208, PLT 215.

260 This is one reason why Heidegger often says that we do not speak language, but language speaks (411). Derrida develops this line of thinking.

261 350, see also 176, 388, PLT 174–5, PLT 216, P 88, N I:144–5, FCM 25, FCM 287.

262 See 349, PLT 217.

263 58, see also 160, 234, 327, 415.

264 350, see also PLT 215.

265 125, see also 333.

266 351, see also PLT 173, PLT 178–80.

267 See 351-52, PLT 178–9.

268 *Being and Time* similarly emphasizes the holistic unity of Dasein's being-in-the-world (see BT 78/53, BT 226/181, BT 275/232, HCT 157), while 'The Origin of the Work of Art' defines earth and world as interdependent (see 174, PLT 202).

269 *Being and Time* makes a similar distinction between Dasein's being-towards-death and animals' perishing (see BT 284–5/241, BT 291/274).

270 See also 168, 242, PLT 229.

271 PLT 220, see also BT 426/374.

272 See 50, 186, 353, PLT 173, PLT 177, PLT 199.

273 355, see also 76–7, 82, 148–51, BT 101/71, BT 132/99, BT 320/275, HCT 83, HCT 86.

274 355, see also PLT 170–1.

275 See 355, PLT 177, PLT 199, PLT 205.

276 See also PLT 174, PLT 179–80, PLT 199–200.

277 See 168, 356, 361, M 23. This discussion bears a strong resemblance to Wallace Stevens's poem, 'Anecdote of a jar'. Placing an unnatural object like a jar in the midst of wilderness fundamentally changes how the whole scene appears. The glass catches our eye, becoming the center of the scene around which everything else is organized. Just as the jar makes the 'wilderness surround that hill', so 'the bridge *gathers* the earth as landscape around the stream' (354).

278 See 348, 361.

279 360, see also FS xvi.

280 357, see also 291, BT 129/96, BT 135–8/102–4, BT 141/106, BT 413/361–2, FS 53.

281 In addition to the phenomenological method of offering a description which captures more of our experience than the 'refuted' view, Heidegger also gives a more logical argument for the priority of lived-space over theoretical space: lived-space can account for and accommodate mere space, but theoretical space can never account for the places we actually live in (357).

282 See BT 377/329, BT 474/422, BT 479/426.

283 See 358–9, BT 140–2/106–7.

284 In related essays, he brings these two phases of his career together by calling the fourfold the world (see PLT 179, PLT 199, PLT 201).

285 359, see also 101–3.

286 PLT 181, see also PLT 200.

287 360, all italics in original, see also 180, 330, STF 148–9, STF 154–5.

288 See 350, 361.

289 See 363, PLT 179. Throughout his career Heidegger shows great indifference to 'ontic' concerns in favour of philosophical issues. Pollution is not the real problem with technology, but our relation to Being. People living on the streets is of less concern than that we do not know how to dwell. He even claims that 'compared to [our encounter with Nietzsche], world wars remain superficial' (PM 321, see also WCT 66, PLT 170).

290 PM 319, see also PLT 185, PLT 223.

291 PLT 190, see also OWL 85, OWL 93, PM 319.

292 The existentialia as opposed to categories (see 59, 66, BT 70/44).

293 See 156–7, 165.

294 See BQ 81, P 55, PM 181–2. I address this topic in greater detail in Braver (2007: 291–303).

295 See 402, OWL 96–7, PLT 192–3, PLT 196, PLT 208, TDP 155, BP 205, BT 201/159, BT 267/224, EGT 77, EGT 91, EGT 99.

296 406, see also PLT 191.

297 See 151–2, BT 207/164, PIS 288, HCT 210, HCT 266, BP 208–9, EGT 64–6, WCT 148–50.

298 See BT 197/155, HCT 263. Bill Blattner suggested this example in conversation.

299 411, see also 78, BT 56/32, BT 196/154, BT 205/162, HCT 262, FCM 309–12, OWL 47, OWL 93, OWL 107, WCT 202, PR 107, MFL 218.

300 411, see also PLT 190, PLT 197–8, PLT 216, PT 25.

301 Wittgenstein in particular never tires of attacking this view of language and the mind in his later work.

302 See 223, 348, 408, 410, 423, PLT 192, PLT 196, PLT 215–16, WCT 128.

303 In *Basic Writings*, 'Letter on Humanism' and 'The Question Concerning Technology' take up this topic at length.

304 411. These themes figure prominently in the work of Derrida (who speaks of his mother tongue as foreign) and Foucault (see, e.g., Foucault (1994: 313; 1996: 52–3), as well as in the school of thought known as structuralism.

305 PLT 216, see also BW 200, OWL 59, OWL 188.

306 See 122, 176–7, 446, BT 261/218–263/220, MFL 127.

307 418, see also OWL 71, OWL 76, PLT 209, PLT 216, PR 96, PT 25.

308 See 188–9, 408, PLT 204–7.

309 410, see also FCM 314–15, FCM 339–40, FCM 346.

310 411, see also 198, 230, PLT 198–9, OWL 65–6, OWL 73, OWL 88, OWL 155, EGT 52, EGT 63–4, EGT 73, EGT 90, OBT 232, M 6, P 76, P 99, P 114, WCT 120, QT 40–1, EHP 55–6.

311   See 411, 413, 416, EGT 66, ID 38–9. The German words for hearing and belonging are very similar.

312   414, see also DT 65.

313   415, see also PLT 179–80, PLT 190–1, WCT 153, WCT 172, FS 59, DT 67.

314   See 397–8, 416, OWL 30, OWL 90, ID 38.

315   See 420–1, WCT 118–19.

316   See 425, PLT 208, OWL 59, WCT 128, EHP 58–60.

317   418, see also 236–7, 262–3, PLT 208, DT 83.

318   At 397–9 and 412–13.

319   413, see also OWL 21, OWL 91.

320   See 167, 170, EHP 36, PLT 192, N I:145.

321   On pages 432 and 436, another example of his helpful signposts.

322   434, see also PM 323, M 44.

323   See 265, 432.

324   432, see also M 283, M 297–8, M 306, M 337, MFL 218–19.

325   435, KPM 193.

326   See FCM 368. Heidegger also briefly alludes to his frequent claim that the end of metaphysics has arrived with 'the uttermost possibility of philosophy' (433), namely Nietzsche's reversal of Plato's founding distinction between the really real timeless unchanging Forms and the temporal, physical collection of things we experience with our senses (see, e.g., OBT 157, OBT 162, OBT 173).

327   See 50–2, 187, 293, 373, 435, 444, FCM 32, FCM 186.

328   See 435, PM 234, PM 335, M 241, OBT 158–9, OBT 196–97, STF 64.

329   We can see fore-shadowings of Derrida's deconstruction here.

330   See PM 332, KPM 140, KPM 175, OBT 133, PR 61, PLT 184.

331   See PM 324, BP 159, EGT 14.

332   See 'My Way to Phenomenology' in OTB (pp. 74–82) for a vivid description of his encounter with this book.

333   Namely, the neo-Kantians who rejected Hegel in order to go 'back to Kant'. See WT 59 and KPM 213–17 for brief discussions.

334   This is quite close to Heidegger's idiosyncratic translation of 'phenomenology', the method shared by both thinkers, in the Introduction of *Being and Time* (see 81).

335   See 227, 234, 443, PM 277, PM 332, M 269.

336   See 235, 446.

337   See 262, 443, KPM 210, PM 277–8, PM 318.

338   448, see also 235, 242, EGT 26, EGT 99, EGT 122, IM 110.

339   OBT 159, see also BW 226, WCT 222, M 146, M 184, M 299.

340   See 103, 126.

341   See 432–3, 446, FS 9, M 206, OBT 58, BQ 47–8, IM 110–11. Gadamer's hermeneutics takes these guidelines to heart.

342   See 437, 448.

343   See 323, N 3:5, N 3:188, N 4:181, QT 54, WCT 46, PR 23–4, PR 87, EGT 19, EGT 55.

344   I address this topic in greater depth in Braver (2007: 339–40).
345   See 435, STF 64, EGT 16.
346   See 436, WCT 159–60, OBT 158, M 74, M 302, PLT 185, PLT 209, PLT 223, DT 62, DT 68.

CHAPTER 4

1   Gadamer (2002: 181).
2   Ibid., 176, 225–6.
3   Foucault (1996: 470).
4   Foucault (2005: 189).
5   One could juxtapose Foucault's 'The Discourse on Language' with Heidegger's 'Modern Science, Mathematics, and Metaphysics' or 'The Age of the World Picture' (in OBT) for a quick, instructive comparison.
6   Derrida (1982: 22).
7   Derrida (1981: 9).

FURTHER READING

The secondary literature on Heidegger continues to grow at an impressive, if not alarming rate. There are a number of very good general purpose collections of essays, including *Heidegger: A Critical Reader* (Dreyfus and Hall, eds.); *A Companion to Heidegger* (Dreyfus and Wrathall, eds.); and *The Cambridge Companion to Heidegger* (Guignon, ed.). The four volume set *Heidegger Reexamined* (Dreyfus and Hall, eds.) reprints many well-regarded essays sorted by topic. *Reading Heidegger: Commemorations* (Sallis, ed.), and *Martin Heidegger: Politics, Art, and Technology* (Harries and Jamme, eds.) are good collections that skew towards the later work.

Otto Pöggeler's *Martin Heidegger's Path of Thinking* and William J. Richardson's *Heidegger: Through Phenomenology to Thought* are considered classic treatments of Heidegger's entire career; Richard Polt's *Heidegger: An Introduction* is a more recent and more introductory discussion that focuses mainly on *Being and Time* but also has short helpful analyses of some later writings.

Among the more specialized treatments, John D. Caputo's *Demythologizing Heidegger* argues that Heidegger's later thought contains a serious internal inconsistency, offering a balance of sympathy, comprehension, and criticism rarely achieved in this secondary literature. Stanley Rosen's *The Question of Being: A Reversal of Heidegger* is a dense critique of Heidegger's conception of metaphysics, especially the way it is grounded in a reading of Plato and Aristotle. I find Michel Haar's works – *Heidegger and the Essence of Man* and *The Song of the Earth: Heidegger and the Grounds of the History of Being* – very stimulating. I would also recommend Reiner Schürmann's *Heidegger – On Being and Acting: From Principles to Anarchy* and Michael E. Zimmerman's *Heidegger's Confrontation with Modernity: Technology, Politics, and Art*. Richard Rorty always makes interesting, even provocative points, and much of his discussion of Heidegger can be found in *Essays on Heidegger and Others: Philosophical Papers Volume 2*.

Those interested in Heidegger's involvement with the Nazi Party would do well to consult Hugo Ott's *Martin Heidegger: A Political Life* and Iain D. Thomson's *Heidegger on Ontotheology: Technology and the Politics of Education*. A more general biography would be Rüdiger Safranski's *Martin Heidegger: Between Good and Evil*.

My own *A Thing of This World: A History of Anti-Realism* (Evanston: Northwestern University Press, 2007) addresses Heidegger's later work at length, showing how it differs from his early work and how it sets the agenda for continental philosophers after him, as well as relating it to various analytic ideas and thinkers. It discusses many of the topics touched on here in greater depth.

Hopefully, this commentary has helped you learn how to read Heidegger's own writings rather than just presenting summaries of his thought. If I have succeeded, readers will find themselves prepared for and interested in reading more of his works, so let me offer a few suggestions. Some works that help illuminate Heidegger's *Kehre* or turn from early to later thought are *The Metaphysical Foundations of Logic*, *The Fundamental Concepts of Metaphysics: World, Finitude, Solitude*, and *Kant and the Problem of Metaphysics*. The Introduction and Postscript to 'What Is Metaphysics?' (in PM), both written later than the essay itself, and *Basic Questions of Philosophy: Selected 'Problems' of 'Logic'* (especially the Appendices) are very helpful discussions of the fundamental investigation of Being. Those interested in Heidegger's engagement with other philosophers should read 'Plato's Doctrine of Truth' (in PM), 'The Age of the World Picture', and 'Nietzsche's Word: "God Is Dead"' (both in OBT). His 1200 pages of lectures on *Nietzsche* are relatively readable (in general, his lectures tend to be more accessible than his writings or talks) and give a nice account of his thoughts on the history of philosophy.

If you liked the discussions of the fourfold in 'Building Dwelling Thinking', then take a look at the essays collected in PLT and OWL. Further discussions of technology occur in essays contained in QT, especially 'The Turning' and 'Science and Reflection'. *What Is Called Thinking?* and *Introduction to Metaphysics* are important works which discuss both earlier philosophers and Heidegger's own project. Some scholars consider *Contributions to Philosophy* to be his second *magnum opus* after *Being and Time*, but I regard it as unfinished (albeit intriguing); many also find its translation problematic. A similar work written right after *Contributions* is *Mindfulness*, which I find much more accessible and interesting. Finally, *The Principle of Reason* remains a personal favorite of mine which deserves more attention.

BIBLIOGRAPHY

WORKS BY MARTIN HEIDEGGER

(2005), *Introduction to Phenomenological Research* (trans. D. O. Dahlstrom). Bloomington: Indiana University Press.

(2003), *Four Seminars* (trans. A. Mitchell and F. Raffoul). Bloomington: Indiana University Press.

(2002), *The Essence of Human Freedom: An Introduction to Philosophy* (trans. T. Sadler). New York: Continuum.

(2002), *The Essence of Truth: On Plato's Cave Allegory and 'Theaetetus'* (trans. T. Sadler). New York: Continuum.

(2002), *Mindfulness* (trans. P. Emad and T. Kalary). New York: Continuum.

(2002), *Off the Beaten Track* (trans. and ed. J. Young and K. Haynes). New York: Cambridge University Press.

(2002), *Supplements: From the Earliest Essays to 'Being and Time' and Beyond* (J. van Buren, ed.). Albany: State University of New York Press.

(2001), *The Fundamental Concepts of Metaphysics: World, Finitude, Solitude* (trans. W. McNeill and N. Walker). Bloomington: Indiana University Press.

(2001), *Zollikon Seminars: Protocols – Conversations – Letters* (trans. F. Mayr and R. Askay). Evanston, IL: Northwestern University Press.

(2000), *Elucidations of Hölderlin's Poetry* (trans. K. Hoeller). Amherst: Humanity Books.

(2000), *Introduction to Metaphysics* (trans. G. Fried and R. Polt). New Haven: Yale University Press.

(2000), *Towards the Definition of Philosophy* (trans. T. Sandler). New York: Athlone.

(1999), *Contributions to Philosophy (From Enowning)* (trans. P. Emad and K. Maly). Bloomington: Indiana University Press.

(1998), *Pathmarks* (W. McNeill, ed.). Cambridge: Cambridge University Press.

(1997), *Phenomenological Interpretation of Kant's 'Critique of Pure Reason'* (trans. P. Emad and T. Kalary). Bloomington: Indiana University Press.

(1997), *Plato's Sophist* (trans. R. Rojcewicz and A. Schuwer). Bloomington: Indiana University Press.

(1996), *Hölderlin's Hymn 'The Ister'* (trans. W. McNeill and J. Davis). Bloomington: Indiana University Press.

(1995), *Aristotle's 'Metaphysics'* Θ *1–3: On the Essence and Actuality of Force* (trans. W. Brogan and P. Warnek). Bloomington: Indiana University Press.

(1994), *Basic Questions of Philosophy: Selected 'Problems' of 'Logic'* (trans. R. Rojcewicz and A. Schuwer). Bloomington: Indiana University Press.

(1994), *Hegel's 'Phenomenology of Spirit'* (trans. P. Emad and K. Maly). Bloomington: Indiana University Press.

(1993), *Basic Concepts* (trans. G. E. Aylesworth). Bloomington: Indiana University Press.

(1993), *Basic Writings* (revised edn, D. F. Krell, ed.). San Francisco: HarperSanFrancisco.

(1993), *Heraclitus Seminar* (coauthored wth E. Fink, trans. C. H. Siebert). Evanston, IL.: Northwestern University Press.

(1992), *The Metaphysical Foundations of Logic* (trans. M. Heim). Bloomington: Indiana University Press.

(1992), *Parmenides* (trans. R. Rojcewicz and A. Schuwer). Bloomington: Indiana University Press.

(1991), *The Principle of Reason* (trans. R. Lilly). Bloomington: Indiana University Press.

(1990), *Kant and the Problem of Metaphysics* (5th enlarged edn., trans. R. Taft). Bloomington: Indiana University Press.

(1985), *History of the Concept of Time* (trans. T. Kisiel). Bloomington: Indiana University Press.

(1985), *Schelling's Treatise on the Essence of Human Freedom* (trans. J. Stambaugh). Athens, OH: Ohio University Press.

(1982), *The Basic Problems of Phenomenology* (trans. A. Hofstadter). Bloomington: Indiana University Press.

(1979, 1984, 1987, 1982), *Nietzsche* 4 vols (D. F. Krell, ed.). San Francisco: HarperSanFrancisco.

(1977), *Martin Heidegger in Conversation* (trans. B. S. Murthy, R. Wisser, ed.). New Delhi: Arnold-Heinemann.

(1977), *The Question Concerning Technology and Other Essays* (trans. W. Lovitt). New York: Harper Torchbooks.

(1976), *The Piety of Thinking* (trans. J. G. Hart and J. C. Maraldo). Bloomington: Indiana University Press.

(1975), *Early Greek Thinking: The Dawn of Western Philosophy* (trans. D. F. Krell and F. A. Capuzzi). San Francisco: HarperSanFrancisco.

(1973), *The End of Philosophy* (trans. J. Stambaugh). New York: Harper and Row.

(1972), *On Time and Being* (trans. J. Stambaugh). New York: Harper Torchbooks.

(1971), *On the Way to Language* (trans. P. D. Hertz). San Francisco: HarperSanFrancisco.

(1971), *Poetry, Language, Thought* (trans. A. Hofstadter). New York: Harper and Row.

(1970), *Hegel's Concept of Experience.* New York: Harper and Row.

(1969), *Identity and Difference* (trans. J. Stambaugh). New York: Harper Torchbooks.

(1968), *What Is Called Thinking?* (trans. J. G. Gray). New York: Harper and Row.

(1967), *What Is a Thing?* (trans. W. B. Barton Jr. and V. Deutsch). Chicago: Henry Regnery.

(1966), *Discourse on Thinking* (trans. J. M. Anderson and E. H. Freund). San Francisco: Harper Torchbooks.

(1962), *Being and Time* (trans. J. Macquarrie and E. Robinson). San Francisco: HarperSanFrancisco.

(1956), *What Is Philosophy?* (trans. J. T. Wilde and W. Kluback). New Haven, Conn.: New College and University Press.

BOOKS BY OTHER AUTHORS

Biemel, W. (1976), *Martin Heidegger: An Illustrated Study.* New York: Harcourt Brace Jovanovich.

Blattner, B. (2006), *Heidegger's Being And Time: A Reader's Guide.* New York: Continuum International Publishing Group.

————. (1999), *Heidegger's Temporal Idealism*. New York: Cambridge University Press.

Braver, L. (2007), *A Thing of This World: A History of Continental Anti-Realism*. Evanston, IL: Northwestern University Press.

Caputo, J. D. (1993), *Demythologizing Heidegger*. Bloomington: Indiana University Press.

Carnap, R. (1959), 'Elimination of Metaphysics Through Logical Analysis of Language', in A. J. Ayer (ed.), *Logical Positivism*. New York: The Free Press, pp. 60–81.

Derrida, J. (1987), *Truth in Painting* (trans. G. Bennington and I. McLeod). Chicago: The University of Chicago Press.

————. (1982), *Margins of Philosophy* (trans. Alan Bass). Chicago: The University of Chicago Press.

————. (1981), *Positions* (trans. A. Bass). Chicago: The University of Chicago Press.

Descartes, R. (1985), 'Discourse on the Method', in J. Cottingham, R. Stoothoff, and D. Murdoch (trans.), *The Philosophical Writings of Descartes* vol. 1. New York: Cambridge University Press.

Dreyfus, H. L. and Hall, H. (eds.). (1992), *Heidegger: A Critical Reader*. Cambridge, Mass: Blackwell Publishers Inc.

Dreyfus, H. L. and Wrathall, M. A. (eds). (2005), *A Companion to Heidegger*. Cambridge, Mass: Blackwell Publishers Inc.

————. (2002), *Heidegger Reexamined*. New York: Routledge.

Foucault, M. (2005), *The Hermeneutics of the Subject: Lectures at the Collège de France 1981–1982* (trans. G. Burchell). New York: Palgrave Macmillan.

————. (1996), *Foucault Live: Collected Interviews, 1961–1984* (2nd edn., S. Lotringer, ed.). New York: Semiotext(e).

————. (1994), *The Order of Things: An Archaeology of Human Sciences*. New York: Vintage Books.

————. (1972), *The Archaeology of Knowledge & The Discourse on Language* (trans. A. M. S. Smith). New York: Harper Colophon Books.

Gadamer, H. -G. (2002), 'Question and answer play back and forth between the text and its interpreter', in D. R. Steele (ed.), *Genius: In Their Own Words*. Open Court: Chicago, pp. 173–238.

Guignon, C. B. (ed.). (2006), *The Cambridge Companion to Heidegger* (2nd edn.). New York: Cambridge University Press.

Haar, M. (1993), *Heidegger and the Essence of Man* (trans. W. McNeill). Albany: State University of New York Press.

———. (1993), *The Song of the Earth: Heidegger and the Grounds of the History of Being* (trans. R. Lilly). Bloomington: Indiana University Press.

Hanson, N. (1958), *Patterns of Discovery*. New York: Cambridge University Press.

Harries, K. and Jamme, C. (eds.). (1994), *Martin Heidegger: Politics, Art, and Technology*. New York: Holmes & Meier Publishers, Inc.,

Kuhn, T. S. (2002), *The Road Since Structure: Philosophical Essays, 1970–1993* (new edn.). Chicago: University of Chicago Press.

———. (1996), *The Structure of Scientific Revolutions* (3rd edn.). Chicago: University of Chicago Press.

Levinas, E. (1996), *Basic Philosophical Writings* (A. T. Peperzak, S. Critchley, and R. Bernasconi, eds). Indianapolis: Indiana University Press.

Nietzsche, F. (1990), *Twilight of the Idols/The Anti-Christ* (trans. R. J. Hollingdale). New York: Penguin Books.

———. (1989a), *Beyond Good and Evil* (trans. W. Kaufmann). New York: Vintage Books.

———. (1989b), *On the Genealogy of Morals/Ecce Homo* (trans. W. Kaufman). New York: Vintage Books.

———. (1968), *The Will to Power* (new edn., trans. W. Kaufman). New York: Vintage Books.

Ott, H. (1993), *Martin Heidegger: A Political Life* (trans. A. Blunden). New York: Basic Books.

Pöggeler, O. (1991), *Martin Heidegger's Path of Thinking* (trans. D. Magurshak and S. Barber). Amherst, NY: Humanity Books.

Polt, R. (1999), *Heidegger: An Introduction*. Ithaca, NY: Cornell University Press.

Richardson, W. J. (2003), *Heidegger: Through Phenomenology to Thought* (4th edn.). New York: Fordham University Press.

Rorty, R. (1991), *Essays on Heidegger and Others: Philosophical Papers Volume 2*. New York: Cambridge University Press.

Rosen, S. (2002), *The Question of Being: A Reversal of Heidegger*. South Bend, Indiana: St. Augustine's Press.

Safranski, R. (1998), *Martin Heidegger: Between Good and Evil* (trans. E. Osers). Cambridge, MA: Harvard University Press.

Sallis, J. (ed.). (1993), *Reading Heidegger: Commemorations*. Bloomington: Indiana University Press.

Sartre, J. -P. (1964), *Nausea* (trans. L. Alexander). New York: New Directions Publishing Corporation.

Schürmann, R. (1990), *Heidegger—On Being and Acting: From Principles to Anarchy* (trans. C. -M. Gros). Bloomington: Indiana University Press.

Sherover, C. M. (1972), *Heidegger, Kant, & Time*. Bloomington: Indiana University Press.

Thomson, I. D. (2005), *Heidegger on Ontotheology: Technology and the Politics of Education*. New York: Cambridge University Press.

Wittgenstein, L. (2001), *Philosophical Investigations* (3rd revised edn., trans. G. E. M. Anscombe). Madsen: Blackwell Publishers Inc.

———. (1993), 'A Lecture on Ethics', in J. Klagge and A. Nordmann (eds.), *Philosophical Occasions 1912–1951*. Indianapolis: Hackett Publishing Company, pp. 36–44.

———. (1988), *Tractatus Logico-Philosophicus* (trans. D. F. Pears and B. F. McGuinness). Atlantic Highlands, NJ.: Humanities Press International, Inc.

Zimmerman, M. E. (1990), *Heidegger's Confrontation with Modernity: Technology, Politics, and Art*. Bloomington: Indiana University Press.

INDEX